The OLD TESTAMENT APOCRYPHA

The OLD TESTAMENT APOCRYPHA

An Introduction

OTTO KAISER

English translation © 2004 by Hendrickson Publishers, Inc.
P. O. Box 3473
Peabody, Massachusetts 01961-3473

ISBN 1-56563-693-7

Translated from Otto Kaiser, *Die alttestamentlichen Apokryphen: Eine Einleitung in Grundzügen,* © 2000, Gütersloher Verlagshaus GmbH, Gütersloh, Germany.

Printed in the United States of America

First Printing — June 2004

Library of Congress Cataloging-in-Publication Data

Kaiser, Otto, 1924–
    [Alttestamentlichen Apokryphen. English]
    The Old Testament Apocrypha : an introduction / Otto Kaiser.
       p. cm.
    Includes bibliographical references.
    ISBN 1-56563-693-7 (alk. paper)
    1. Bible. O.T. Apocrypha—Introductions.   I. Title.
    BS1700.K2713 2004
    229'.061—dc22
                    2004005916

Table of Contents

Frequently Cited Works

Eißfeldt, O. *The Old Testament: An Introduction.* 3d ed. New York: Harper & Row, 1965 (= Eißfeldt, *Introduction*).

Kaiser, O. *Der Gott des Alten Testaments. Theologie des AT 1: Grundlegung.* UTB 1747. Göttingen: Vandenhoeck & Ruprecht, 1993 (= *GAT* I).

————. *Der Gott des Alten Testaments. Theologie des AT 2: Werden und Wirken.* UTB 2024. Göttingen: Vandenhoeck & Ruprecht, 1998 (= *GAT* II).

Oesterley, W. O. E. *An Introduction to the Books of the Apocrypha.* London: S.P.C.K., 1958 (= *Introduction*).

Rost, L. *Einleitung in die alttestamentlichen Apokryphen und Pseudepigraphen einschließlich der großen Qumran-Handschriften.* Heidelberg: Quelle & Meyer, 1971 (= Rost, *EinlApo*).

Schürer, E. *The History of the Jewish People in the Age of Jesus Christ (175 B.C.–A.D. 135): A New English Version.* 3 vols. in 4. G. Vermes et al., rev. and ed. T. Burkill et al., trans. Edinburgh: T&T Clark, 1973–1987 (= Schürer/Vermes 1–3.2).

Zenger, E., ed. *Einleitung in das Alte Testament.* KStTh 1/1. 3d ed. Stuttgart: Kohlhammer, 1998 (= Zenger, *Einleitung*).

For additional abbreviations, see Abbreviations on the next page.

Abbreviations

BTT	Blackwell's Theological Texts
BWANT	Beiträge zur Wissenschaft vom Alten und Neuen Testament
BZ	*Biblische Zeitschrift*
BZAW	Beihefte zur Zeitschrift für die alttestamentliche Wissenschaft
BZNW	Beihefte zur Zeitschrift für die neutestamentliche Wissenschaft
ConBNT	Coniectanea biblica: New Testament Series
CBC	Cambridge Bible Commentary
CBQ	*Catholic Biblical Quarterly*
CBQMS	Catholic Biblical Quarterly Monograph Series
DDD	*Dictionary of Deities and Demons in the Bible.* Ed. K. van der Toorn, Bob Becking, and P. W. van der Horst. Leiden, 1995
DJD	Discoveries in the Judaean Desert
EB	Echter Bibel
EBib	Etudes bibliques
EHAT	Exegetisches Handbuch zum Alten Testament
EHST	Europäische Hochschulschriften, Reihe 23, Theologie
EvT	*Evangelische Theologie*
ETS	Erfurter theologische Studien
FARG	Forschungen zur Anthropologie und Religionsgeschichte
FB	Forschung zur Bibel
FOTL	Forms of the Old Testament Literature
FRLANT	Forschungen zur Religion und Literatur des Alten und Neuen Testaments
GAT	Grundrisse zum Alten Testament
GAT I–II	*Der Gott des Alten Testaments.* By O. Kaiser. 2 vols. Göttingen, 1993–1998.
GGPh	Grundriss der Geschichte der Philosophie
GL	De Gruyter Lehrbuch
GS	Geistliche Schriftlesung
HAT	Handbuch zum Alten Testament
HAW	Handbuch der Altertumswissenschaft
HBK	Die heilige Schrift für das Leben erklärt
HBS	Herders biblische Studien
HDR	Harvard Dissertations in Religion
Herm	Hermeneia
HSAT	*Die Heilige Schrift des Alten Testaments.* Ed. E. Kautzsch and A. Bertholet. 4th ed. Tübingen, 1922–1923

HSM	Harvard Semitic Monographs
HSS	Harvard Semitic Studies
HTR	*Harvard Theological Review*
HTS	Harvard Theological Studies
HUCA	*Hebrew Union College Annual*
JAL	Jewish Apocryphal Literature Series
JBL	*Journal of Biblical Literature*
JJS	*Journal of Jewish Studies*
JNSL	*Journal of Northwest Semitic Languages*
JQR	*Jewish Quarterly Review*
JSHRZ	Jüdische Schriften aus hellenistisch-römischer Zeit
JSJ	*Journal for the Study of Judaism in the Persian, Hellenistic, and Roman Periods*
JSOTSup	Journal for the Study of the Old Testament: Supplement Series
JSPSup	Journal for the Study of the Pseudepigrapha Supplement Series
JSS	*Journal of Semitic Studies*
KStTh	Kohlhammer Studienbücher: Theologie
MdB	Le Monde de la Bible
MPIL	Monographs of the Peshitta Institute of Leiden
NAWG	Nachrichten von der Akademie der Wissenschaften in Göttingen
NEchtB	Neue Echter Bibel
NEchtB.EAT	Neue Echter Bibel, Ergänzungsband zum Alten Testament
Neot	*Neotestamentica*
NGWG	Nachrichten der Gesellschaft der Wissenschaften zu Göttingen
NJBC	*The New Jerome Bible Commentary.* Ed. Raymond Brown et al. Englewood Cliffs, 1990.
NRTh	*La nouvelle revue théologique*
NSKAT	Neuer Stuttgarter Kommentar zum Alten Testaments
NTApo	*New Testament Apocrypha.* Ed. E. Hennecke and W. Schneemelcher. 3d ed. 2 vols. London, 1964.
NTOA	Novum Testamentum et Orbis Antiquus
NTS	*New Testament Studies*
OBO	Orbis biblicus et orientalis
OGG	Oldenbourg Grundriss der Geschichte
OTL	Old Testament Library
OTP	*Old Testament Pseudepigrapha.* Ed. J. H. Charlesworth. 2 vols. New York, 1983

PTA	Papyrologische Texte und Abhandlungen
PVTG	Pseudepigrapha Veteris Testamenti Graece
RB	*Revue biblique*
RHPR	*Revue d'histoire et de philosophie religieuses*
RevQ	*Revue de Qumran*
RivB	*Revista biblica italiana*
RSR	*Recherches de science religieuse*
SANT	Studien zum Alten und Neuen Testaments
SB	La Sacra Bibbia
SBAB	Stuttgarter biblische Aufsatzbände
SBB	Stuttgarter biblische Beiträge
SBJ	La Sainte Bible traduite en francais sous la direction de l'Ecole Biblique de Jerusalem
SBLDS	Society of Biblical Literature Dissertation Series
SBLEJL	Society of Biblical Literature Early Judaism and Its Literature
SBLMS	Society of Biblical Literature Monograph Series
SBLSCS	Society of Biblical Literature Septuagint and Cognate Studies
SBS	Stuttgarter Bibelstudien
SIJB	Schriften Institutum Judaicum, Berlin
SJLA	Studies in Judaism in Late Antiquity
SNVAO	Skrifter utgitt av Det Norske Videnskaps-Akademi i Oslo
SR	Studies in Religion
SSS	Semitic Studies Series
STDJ	Studies on the Texts of the Desert of Judah
StPB	Studia post-biblica
SUNT	Studien zur Umwelt des Neuen Testaments
SVF	*Stoicorum veterum fragmenta.* By H. von Arnim. 4 vols. Leipzig, 1903–24.
SVTP	Studia in Veteris Testamenti pseudepigraphica
ThSt	Theologische Studien
ThW	Theologische Wissenschaft
TLZ	*Theologische Literaturzeitung*
TRE	*Theologische Realenzyklopädie.* Ed. G. Krause and G. Müller. Berlin, 1977–
TSAJ	Texte und Studien zum antiken Judentum
TThSt	Trierer theologische Studiën
TTZ	*Trierer theologische Zeitschrift*
TU	Texte und Untersuchungen
UBL	Ugaritisch-biblische Literatur

UTB	Uni-Taschenbücher
VF	Verkündigung und Forschung
VT	*Vetus Testamentum*
VTSup	Vetus Testamentum Supplements
VWGT	Veröffentlichungen der Wissenschaftlichen Gesellschaft für Theologie
WD	*Wort und Dienst*
WMANT	Wissenschaftliche Monographien zum Alten und Neuen Testament
WUNT	Wissenschaftliche Untersuchungen zum Neuen Testament
ZDMG	*Zeitschrift der deutschen morgenländischen Gesellschaft*
ZDPV	*Zeitschrift des deutschen Palästina-Vereins*
ZNW	*Zeitschrift für die neutestamentliche Wissenschaft und die Kunde der älteren Kirche*
ZRGG	*Zeitschrift für Religions- und Geistesgeschichte*
ZTK	*Zeitschrift für Theologie und Kirche*

1

Introduction

The Deutercanonical Books or Apocrypha

The terms "Deuterocanonical books" or "Old Testament Apocrypha" refer to the Jewish documents that originated between the third century B.C.E. and the first century C.E. and that were incorporated into the Greek but not the Hebrew Bible.[1] They are: Judith, the Wisdom of Solomon, Tobias or Tobit, the book of Jesus ben Sirach or Ecclesiasticus, the book of Baruch with the Letter of Jeremiah, 3 Ezra, 1 and 2 Maccabees, the Additions to the Greek book of Esther, and the Additions to the Greek book of Daniel (consisting of the stories of Susanna and Daniel and of Bel and the Dragon in Babylon, the Prayer of Azariah, the Song of the three men in the fiery furnace), and finally the late Prayer of Manasseh. The three Christian churches hold differing attitudes toward these books even today.

The Decisions of the Three Major Christian churches

The Western Roman Catholic Church recognized them as canonical in their synods at Hippo (393 C.E.), Carthage (397; see DS 179; again in 419), renewed this decision at the Union Council of Florence (1442; DS 1335), and ratified it in session IV of the Council of Trent (1546; DS 1501–5),[2] while continuing to transmit 3 and 4 Ezra, Psalm 151, and the Letter to the Laodiceans in the Vulgate in an appendix after the New Testament. The Orthodox Church reached a similar decision at the Council of Jerusalem (1672), which recognized the Apocrypha as books of equal

---

[1] In the early church, for example, Athanasius distinguished in his thirty-ninth festal letter between the books of the Hebrew Bible as canonical, those contained only in the Greek as "the others beside these," which were nonetheless suitable for reading, and the apocrypha now categorized as pseudepigrapha (see H.-P. Rüger, "Apokryphen I: Die Apokryphen des Alten Testaments," *TRE* 3:291–92).

[2] According to this council, the church "should accept and venerate with a disposition of piety and reverence . . . all the books of both Old and New Testaments, each with one God as its author."

value with the Holy Scripture and, in addition to the books named above, included the Odes and 3 Maccabees.[3] In the same year, the Synod of Constantinople explicitly confirmed this decision and determined that the Old Testament contains 33 books.[4]

The Lutheran and Reformed Churches decided otherwise. Luther judged the Apocrypha not to be of equal value with the other books of Holy Scripture and, therefore, excluded them from the canon. They appeared in his 1534 and 1545 editions of the Bible as an appendix under the heading "Apocrypha: These are books, although not considered Holy Scripture, which are nonetheless useful and good to read."[5] The Reformed Church did not differ in the Belgic Confession, Art. 6 (1562),[6] nor did the Anglican Church, also in Article 6 of the *Thirty-nine Articles of Religion* from the same year.[7] Thereby the books of the Apocrypha lost their significance in Protestantism for church doctrine and proclamation. Apart from the academic attention sometimes afforded them, they came to serve, at best only for private edification and instruction. Until the middle of the twentieth century, they were increasingly forgotten.

The Deuterocanonical Writings in the Interplay between Judaism and Hellenism

Objectively, there can be little doubt that the writings named above are best categorized as deuterocanonical, because they presuppose the validity of the Law and the Prophets and also utilize the *Ketûbîm* or "Writings" collection which was, at the time, still in the process of formation and not yet closed.[8] They offer us, therefore, a glimpse of how, in an in-

---

[3] See the text in A. P. Chastoupes, *Eisagoge eis ten Palaian Diatheken* (Athens: Christanike, 1981), 560–61.

[4] Chastoupes, *Eisagoge*, 561–62.

[5] H. Volz, ed. *Die Übersetzung des Apokryphenteils des Alten Testaments* (Martin Luthers Werke: Kritische Gesamtausgabe 12; Weimar: Böhlau, 1961), 2–3, 290–91. In his introductions to the individual books, Luther certified them all—except for Baruch, which he did not translate and thus merely borrowed from another translation, and 3 Ezra, which along with 4 Ezra he passed over—as useful for the faith and life of the Christian.

[6] See W. Niesel, *Bekenntnisschriften und Kirchenordnungen der nach Gottes Wort reformierten Kirche* (2d ed.; Zürich: Evangelischer Verlag, 1939), 121:10–30; cited also in Rüger, "Apokryphen I," 294.

[7] John Leith, ed., *Creeds of the Church* (3d ed.; Atlanta: John Knox, 1982), 267–69.

[8] Today, thanks to the documents discovered in the eleven caves at Qumran and in the Judean Desert, in addition to knowledge of the pseudepigrapha included in individual manuscripts of the Septuagint, we are better informed than ever concerning the scope of the Jewish religious literature originating in the Hellenistic-Roman period; see J. C. VanderKam, *The Dead Sea Scrolls Today* (Grand Rapids: Eerdmans, 1994), 29–70.

creasingly hellenized environment, Judaism, both in Palestine and in the Egyptian and West Asian Diaspora, gave account of its faith in its divine election and of the associated duty to obedience to the Torah or instruction of its God. In this way, it reworked the old biblical themes along with those of its historical direction and dispensations. Here expectations of the judgment of the nations that would finally reverse Israel's exilic fate transformed into expectations of the judgment of the world and, later, of the Last Judgment for the living and the dead. In its expectation, finally, the prophetic and wisdom traditions, once separately transmitted and received, united under the canopy of the unassailable demand for total obedience to the law. This process is only partially reflected in the latest redactions of the prophetic books, in the Psalms, and to a lesser extent in the wisdom writings of the books later included in the Hebrew Bible.[9]

The influence of the Hellenistic environment is evident even in conservative circles that adhered to the Torah and considered all expectations beyond its promises and threats as superfluous. As can be observed in the Wisdom of Jesus ben Sirach, active sometime between 195 and 185 B.C.E., the coexistence of general wisdom in circulation among all nations, the Jewish Torah, and especially the pedagogical proverbial wisdom achieved a reasonable accommodation. Sirach completed it by declaring the Lord to be the source of all wisdom and the Torah to be the totality of divine wisdom and the uncreated wellspring of wisdom. The observance of it teaches human beings to fear God and to keep the rules of prudence as presented in the empirical wisdom anchored in human creatureliness. Furthermore, he utilized the Stoic concepts of divine providence and of the beauty and rationality of the whole, of which every individual is a necessary part, in order to undergird belief in the perfection of the works and the inscrutability of God's wisdom.

The Transcendence of Israel's God, God's Uniqueness, and the Belief in the Mediation of Angels

If we turn to the deuterocanonical books, we observe, on the one hand, how God is conceived ever more clearly in terms of superiority to the world and, relatedly, of remoteness from the world of human beings.

---

[9] See, for example, O. H. Steck, *Der Abschluß der Prophetie im Alten Testament: Ein Versuch zur Frage der Vorgeschichte des Kanons* (BThSt 17; Neukirchen-Vluyn: Neukirchener Verlag, 1991); and regarding the exegetical process inherent in the redactions, O. H. Steck, *Die Prophetenbücher und ihr theologisches Zeugnis: Wege der Nachfrage und Fährten zur Antwort* (Tübingen: Mohr, 1996), 145–86; Kaiser, *GAT* I, 231–62.

On the other hand, we note how the realm between heaven and earth simultaneously becomes the realm of angels as God's messengers and reciprocal mediators between human beings and the distant God, inaccessible in his holiness.[10] In the book of Tobit we encounter in most attractive form belief in the archangels, who always have access to God, who bring people's prayers before him, and whom he sends as helping guides to supplicants. At the same time, we perceive the practical Torah piety that appeals to the Golden Rule and feels obligated to practice acts of mercy, feeding the hungry, clothing the naked, and burying the dead. Even under persecution, it adheres to obedience to God's will, submits to him in life and death, and, therefore, experiences his wondrous direction and leading. Under the influence of the Hellenistic spirit, systematization and hierarchization arise here, too.[11] Thus, for example, in the Book of the Watchers in 1 Enoch 1–36 one finds it much more vibrant. The four or seven archangels stand in contrast to those angels who have decided to mix with the human women, teach humans all the harmful arts, beget with them the legendary giants, and thus remain imprisoned for their crimes until the last days. Certain partially overlapping tasks are attributed to the archangels. Just how the heavenly host multiplies, how the prince of light with his host contrasts to the angel of darkness with his,[12] and how the pious imagination devises the hymns that the angels in heaven sing at sacrifices, we learn from the Qumran documents.[13]

The situation is more settled, but in the end no less wondrous, in the Diaspora narratives of Susanna and the clever Daniel and of Bel and the Dragon. Like the stories in Dan 2–6, they attest to an undisturbed relationship with pagan authority and, at the same time, to an uncompromising fidelity to the first commandment. The young Daniel already shows his own superiority as the defender of the innocence of a maliciously accused virgin, and he shows God to be the one who hears the prayer of the innocent. As a courtier called to account by his king, the Persian Cyrus II, for refusing to bow to the idol of Bel although Bel was a living god, he contradicts his lord's heresy by exposing the priests' deceit. Thus, he could have even read the pseudepigraphical Epistle of Jeremiah written to those deported to Babylon (a document often included as the sixth chapter of 1 Baruch, as in the Luther Bible), in which

---

[10] See also Kaiser, GAT II, 152–60.

[11] See M. Hengel, Judaism and Hellenism (Philadelphia: Fortress, 1974), 228–41.

[12] See H. Stegemann, The Library of Qumran: On the Essenes, Qumran, John the Baptist, and Jesus (Grand Rapids: Eerdmans, 1998), 202–4; or J. J. Collins, Apocalypticism in the Dead Sea Scrolls (New York: Routledge, 1997), 38–51.

[13] See Collins, Apocalypticism, 136–43; or VanderKam, Dead Sea Scrolls Today, 60–64.

the prophet urges them not to fear the dumb idols of human manufacture. Commanded by the king to pray to the dragon as the living god, Daniel demonstrates its invalidity by poisoning it and thereby causing it to burst. When the king reluctantly yields to popular pressure and has Daniel thrown into the lion's den, the prophet Habakkuk, transported by an angel from Judea to Babylon especially for this purpose, cares for him. Even more wondrous is the situation in the narrative framing the Prayer of Azariah and the Song of the Three Young Men in the fiery furnace, in which an angel sees to it that the flames spare Daniel's three friends but consume their tormentors.

In contrast, the people in the Judith story, which has elements of the erotic Hellenistic novel, depend entirely upon themselves and upon God. Thanks to her unshakeable faith in God and to make it apparent that the Lord is the only God, the beautiful but honorable widow decapitates General Holofernes, come to destroy the Jerusalem temple and to assert Nebuchadnezzar's claim to be the only god on earth.

In its glorification of the deeds of the Maccabees—Mattathias and his sons Judas Maccabee, Jonathan, and Simon, and his grandson John Hyrcanus—1 Maccabees relies on the methods of classical biblical historiography, forgoing all miraculous elements. The new piety is apparent, however, in the interpretation of all victories as the divine response to the preceding prayer of the hero. In the same spirit, the editors of the books of Esther and Daniel placed prayers to the Lord on the lips of their heroes, Mordecai and Esther or Azariah and Daniel's three friends, respectively, before their decisive acts or in their times of need.

Matters differ entirely in 2 Maccabees as a good example of Judeo-Hellenistic historiography. It participates in the preference of contemporary Hellenistic historiography for the appearance and intervention of heavenly beings in earthly conflicts. For example, they mortally wound Chancellor Seleucus IV Heliodorus, who had wantonly intruded into the temple.[14] Before his decisive battle with General Demetrios I Nicanor, the high priest Onias appeared to Judas in a dream as Israel's intercessor while the prophet Jeremiah handed him a golden, holy sword with which he would shatter his enemies.[15] Before the battle, Judas reminded God that his angel had saved Hezekiah from Sennacherib's superior force, and entreated him to send a good angel now, too, who would teach the enemies to fear.[16]

---

[14] 2 Macc 3:23–39.
[15] 2 Macc 15:12–16.
[16] 2 Macc 15:22–23.

The Historical Background

One must keep in view the waxing and waning expectations of the pious who, since Alexander the Great's victorious campaign, had awaited the judgment of the world. Yet, instead of the judgment of the world that would mean the end of foreign domination, merely another ruler, another dynasty, or another nation assumed dominion over Jerusalem and Judah. Out of the struggles among the Diadochoi arose the three great Hellenistic monarchies: the Antigonids in the Greco-Macedonian motherland, the Seleucids over Asia, and the Ptolemies over Egypt. Contrary to the will of the victors in the decisive defeat of the final generals seeking overall dominion, Antigonus Monophthalmos (the "one-eyed") and his son Demetrios Polyorketes (the "city-subduer"), Ptolemy I took possession of Coele Syria and Phoenicia (including Palestine) in the year 301. Thereupon, the Seleucids, defrauded of a portion of their realm, sought in the five Syrian Wars fought between 274 and 200 B.C.E. to assert their legal claims and to regain the province of Coele Syria and Phoenicia, which Antiochus III was only able to do in the final war in this series. Yet, conquered by the Romans and deprived of his territories in Asia Minor, he left his heirs with the burden of the war indemnity owed the victor. Thus, the basis was established for the unfortunate transaction involving the office of the Jerusalem high priest. King Antiochus IV was moved to insist on his high priest, Menelaus, whom the pious rejected, and to issue the unfortunate religious edict that resulted in the successful rebellion of the Maccabees.

While the Seleucid Kingdom gradually dissolved with the distinctly more remote but effective assistance of the rulers of Pergamon and especially of the Romans, the Hasmoneans, now risen to the high-priestly office, pursued an adroit zigzag course between the true and the pretended claimants to the Seleucid throne until they gained outright independence in 141 B.C.E. Beginning at the end of the second century, they called themselves kings in diplomatic correspondence with other powers and, indeed, controlled a kingdom as large as King David's. In the end, theirs may even have exceeded his.

When their dynasty collapsed in fraternal discord, Rome, represented by Pompey, laid its inexorable hand on the land, conquered Jerusalem in 63 B.C.E., and deported the energetic Aristobulus II, who had driven his brother from the high priesthood and declared himself king, to Rome. His brother, Hyrcanus II, ceded power to his Edomite majordomo, Antipater, who, with no less skill than his son Herod later, understood how to steer the Jewish ship of state through the waves of the Roman civil war that had reached Palestine. Hyrcanus also warded off the attempts of Aristobulus II and his sons, Alexander and Antigonus, to win back the lost crown. Unloved by the Jewish people, Herod the Great remained king by Rome's grace. Despite the extent of his realm and the privileges granted him by Julius Caesar and Augustus, the middle period of his reign was plagued by his more-or-less well-founded mistrust of his young, beloved brother-in-law, Aristobulus III—holder of the high priesthood, grandson of Hyrcanus II, and brother of his wife Mariamne—of the aged grandfather of both his wife and her brother, and finally also of Hyrcanus's other grandson and his sons, Alexander and Antigonus. Eventually he liquidated them all in sequence. When, seven days before his own death, he also had Antipater, his favorite son from his first marriage, poisoned, the inner catastrophe of his externally so successful life was complete. Yet when he died, he left behind a changed country: the rebuilding of the temple that he began, his palaces, newly-founded cities, and his mountaintop mausoleum gave the country luster. In accordance with his will, his kingdom was divided among his three sons, Archelaus, Herod Antipas, and Philip. Nevertheless, in the hearts of the pious, for whom the pagan character of their ruler was an abomination, hope for the coming of the kingdom of God and his anointed grew. The hope that began as a spark in the middle of the second century B.C.E. was fanned into an ever-burning flame.[17]

The Development of Jewish Eschatology

The book of Baruch demonstrates the continued vitality, even in Hellenistic Judaism, of the classical expectation of the return to Zion of the

---

[17] For the Hellenistic and Roman history of the period, see the brief, but comprehensive H.-J. Gehrke, *Geschichte des Hellenismus* (OGG 1A; Munich: Oldenbourg, 1990); and the relevant chapters in J. Bleicken, *Römische Republik* (4th ed.; OGG 2; Munich: Oldenbourg, 1992); for the Jewish history, see the portrayal by W. O. E. Oesterley, *A History of Israel II: From the Fall of Jerusalem, 586 B.C. to the Bar-Kokhba Revolt, A.D. 135* (Oxford: Clarendon, 1957), which, despite its age, is still useful for an understanding of the political history; the exhaustive anthology by W. D. Davies und L. Finkelstein, eds. *The Cambridge History of Judaism, vol. 2: The Hellenistic Age* (Cambridge: Cambridge University Press, 1989); the works (current, but each dealing with only a specific topic) by Hengel, *Judaism and Hellenism* or Schürer/Vermes 1; or the corresponding chapters in A. H. J. Gunneweg, *Geschichte Israels: Von den Anfängen bis Bar Kochba und von Theodor Herzl bis zur Gegenwart* (6th ed.; ThW 2; Stuttgart: Kohlhammer, 1989); J. Maier, *Zwischen den Testamenten: Geschichte und Religion in der Zeit des Zweiten Tempels* (NEchtB.EAT 3; Würzburg: Echter, 1990); or H. Donner, *Geschichte des Volkes Israel und seiner Nachbarn in Grundzügen II: Von der Königszeit bis zu Alexander dem Großen: Mit einem Ausblick auf die Geschichte des Judentums bis Bar Kochba* (2d ed.; GAT; Göttingen: Vandenhoeck & Ruprecht, 1995).

exiled and dispersed and of the glory of the New Jerusalem as a consequence of the downfall of its enemies. The desire for the universal acknowledgement of the Lord by all peoples of the world is reflected in the
conversion of the Ammonite Achior/Ahikar to Judaism[18] and in King
Artaxerxes' indirect confession of the God of the Jews. Countermanding
the previous decree calling for the murder of the Jews (inserted in G after
Esth 8:12), he declares that "God, who rules over all things," has transformed their day of destruction into a day of rejoicing (E v. 22).

God's mill, however, grinds slowly and not in such a way that belief in
his righteousness in earthly events makes sense to everyone. In an age in
which cities and small states lost power, depoliticization, individualiza-
tion, and introspection were inevitable. They also appear in the withdrawal of the pious Jew from a world where the righteous often suffer and
the godless transgressor triumphs.[19] Regarding the question of the reason
for the delay of the promised salvation, one of the final editors of the book
of Isaiah had already, at or just outside the threshold of Hellenism, an-
swered that the hand of the Lord is not too short to help, but sin separates
one from God.[20] Thus the pious joined together, first loosely, and then by
the middle of the 70s of the second century B.C.E. more closely, in organized societies whose goal was to atone for Israel's guilt through their fidelity to the law and piety. Nonetheless, the coming of salvation continued
to be further delayed. Thus, in the course of the third century B.C.E., the
pious became receptive to the message of Greco-Hellenistic mystery religions concerning the judgment of the dead and transformed it into the expectation of universal judgment on the living and the dead. Some were to
be condemned to eternal shame, but others would be destined for eternal
life. Awakened from the dust, their souls will ascend to the world of heavenly light. The Book of the Watchers (*1 En.* 1–36) proclaims these expectations as a novelty, and the Enoch letter (*1 En.* 91–105), as comfort for the
pious. Such hopes are mirrored, for example, in Dan 12:1–3.

Around the middle of the second century, the formation of the three
religious parties whose names are familiar to the reader of the New Testament began: the Essene community as the strictest group obligated to
priestly purity and holiness,[21] the Pharisees[22] as comparatively more lib-

---

[18] Jdt 14:5–10.

[19] See Ps 39:2; 73:1–28; Isa 57:1–2.

[20] Isa 59:1–15.

[21] Concerning their history and doctrine, see Stegemann, *Library of Qumran*, 139–210;
Schürer/Vermes 2:555–90; or Maier, *Testamenten*, 272–83. According to Hartmut Stegemann (orally), the scribes of the Gospels represent the Essenes.

[22] See Schürer/Vermes 2:381–403; Maier, *Testamenten*, 268–72.

eral interpreters of the Torah, and the Sadducees.[23] In accordance with their origin in the assembly of the Hasidim, the Essenes and the Pharisees shared their eschatological-apocalyptic expectations. These expectations received new nourishment from the persecution and killing of many pious individuals in the days of the religious persecution ordered by Antiochus IV at the instigation of the high priest Menelaus.[24] The next high priest, Alcimus, also assaulted a large number of the devout at least once (1 Macc 7:13–18; see 2 Macc 14). The conflict burned most intensely, however, between the Pharisees and King Alexander Jannaeus. Josephus reports that he arrested six thousand festival pilgrims at a Succoth festival (*Ant.* 13.373–374). Later, after his final victory over the Seleucid king Demetrios III Eucarios (95–88 B.C.E.), who had been summoned by his Jewish enemies presumably at the instigation of the Pharisees, he allegedly had eight hundred of his opponents crucified after the slaughter of their wives and children (*Ant.* 12.379–383), an act that prompted thousands of Jews to flee abroad. As a result, Pompey's termination of the Hasmonean monarchy in 63 B.C.E., seemed to the pious (as we learn from *Pss. Sol.* 8) to be the fitting judgment of God. Pompey's own end, moreover, seemed the deserved penalty for his profanation of the temple (*Pss. Sol.* 2).

The expectation of eternal life awaiting the righteous and eternal destruction awaiting the transgressor is so self-evident for the Songs edited shortly after his death in 48 B.C.E. that the mere mention of the mythological motif suffices. *Psalms of Solomon 17* demonstrates that individual hope had not supplanted collective hope. It asks God to awaken a king for Israel from the house of David so that he may chasten Israel's enemies, cleanse Jerusalem, and lead his people to righteousness. We do not learn how one expectation relates to the other. Presumably, the Pharisaic poets were still so bound by aspectual thinking that they did not recognize the problem.

The Wisdom of Solomon, which presumably originated in the early Augustan period, demonstrates how these expectations, evidenced especially in the pseudepigraphical apocalypses, spread as a matter of course even in Alexandrian Judaism. If one looks back on the lively account— probably from the mid-second-century Alexandria and transmitted by Josephus in *Ant.* 12.160–234—of the two Tobiads, Joseph and his son Hyrcanus, as examples of successful Jewish assimilation to modern culture and attitudes, then the contrast with their counterpart, the conservative

---

[23] See Schürer/Vermes 2:404–14; Maier, *Testamenten*, 257–59.
[24] See K. Bringmann, *Hellenistische Reform und Religionsverfolgung in Judäa: Eine Untersuchung zur jüdisch-hellenistischen Geschichte (175–163 v.Chr.)* (AAWG 3.132; Göttingen: Vandenhoeck & Ruprecht, 1983).

high priest Onias,[25] could not be sharper. To be sure, the author of Wisdom can in fact assume that his readers have the requisite biblical and Hellenistic education when he delivers his message with all the tools of late Hellenistic rhetoric and literary language. Meanwhile cultural optimism has subsided; the world has become darker. The shadows of the persecution of the pious from the days of Antiochus IV to Alexander Jannaeus seem to extend to Alexandria. Thus it seemed to the author time (1) to oppose the purposeless hedonism of his day with the message of righteousness grounded in obedience to the Torah as the prerequisite for immortality and with the reassessment of all traditional values in light of the message of the rapture of the souls of the righteous from the underworld to the world of heavenly light and the horrific end of the godless; (2) to recommend to them true God-given wisdom; and, (3) as comfort for the pious, to show them scriptural evidence of how helpful wisdom has proven to be in Israel's history and how righteous God is. Now the issue is no longer assimilation but that the externally assimilated remain Jews internally. Meanwhile, these Jews know the apocalyptic eschatological expectations so well that mere allusions suffice to call them to mind. At the same time, the author of Wisdom of Solomon puts his knowledge of philosophical theology, a middle way between Stoicism and Platonism (like that attested in Posidonius), to demonstrate that Israel knows the true God.[26] Thus, in their fashion, the Wisdom of Jesus ben Sirach and the Wisdom of Solomon demonstrate that the beginnings of theology are apologetic in nature. It retains this character so long as it understands what it means that its faith is a faith under attack, a faith inexpressible apart from the spirit of its time but that can hope to assure itself in dialog with its time—to hope, not to know, because faith is a gift of the Spirit.

Bibliography

Introductions:

H.-P. Rüger, "Apokryphen I: Die Apokryphen des Alten Testaments." Pages 289–316 in vol. 3 of *Theologische Realenzyklopädie.* Edited by G. Krause and G. Müller. New York: de Gruyter, 1978 (with an introduction to the documents included among the apocrypha).

---

[25] See Hengel, *Judaism and Hellenism,* 267–72.
[26] Wis 13:1–9.

Issues:

W. O. E. Oesterley. *A History of Israel II: From the Fall of Jerusalem, 586 B.C. to the Bar-Kokhba Revolt, A.D. 135.* 1932. Repr., Oxford: Clarendon, 1957.

————. *An Introduction to the Books of the Apocrypha.* 1935. Repr., London: S.P.C.K., 1958.

M. Hengel. *Judaism and Hellenism.* Philadelphia: Fortress, 1974.

Schürer/Vermes 1–3.2.

A. P. Chastoupes, *Eisagoge eis ten Palaian Diatheken.* Athens: Christanike, 1981.

K. Bringmann. *Hellenistische Reform und Religionsverfolgung in Judäa: Eine Untersuchung zur jüdisch-hellenistischen Geschichte (175–163 v.Chr.).* AAWG 3/132. Göttingen: Vandenhoeck & Ruprecht, 1983.

P. Schäfer. *Geschichte der Juden in der Antike: Die Juden Palästinas von Alexander dem Großen bis zur arabischen Eroberung.* Stuttgart: Katholisches Bibelwerk, 1983.

O. Kaiser. *Der Mensch unter dem Schicksal: Studien zur Geschichte, Theologie und Gegenwartsbedeutung der Weisheit.* BZAW 161. New York: de Gruyter, 1985.

————. *GAT* I.

————. *GAT* II.

————. *Gottes und der Menschen Weisheit.* BZAW 261. New York: de Gruyter, 1998.

W. D. Davies and L. Finkelstein, eds. *The Hellenistic Age.* Vol. 2 of *The Cambridge History of Judaism.* Cambridge: Cambridge University Press, 1989.

A. H. J. Gunneweg. *Geschichte Israels: Von den Anfängen bis Bar Kochba und von Theodor Herzl bis zur Gegenwart.* 6th ed. ThW 2. Stuttgart: Kohlhammer, 1989.

J. Maier. *Zwischen den Testamenten: Geschichte und Religion in der Zeit des Zweiten Tempels.* NEchtB.EAT 3. Würzburg: Echter, 1990.

H.-J. Gehrke. *Geschichte des Hellenismus.* OGG 1A. Munich: Oldenbourg, 1990.

O. H. Steck. *Der Abschluß der Prophetie im Alten Testament: Ein Versuch zur Frage der Vorgeschichte des Kanons.* BThSt 17. Neukirchen-Vluyn: Neukirchener Verlag, 1991.

————. *Die Prophetenbücher und ihr theologisches Zeugnis: Wege der Nachfrage und Fährten zur Antwort.* Tübingen: Mohr, 1996.

J. Bleicken. *Geschichte der römischen Republik.* 4th ed. OGG 2. Munich: Oldenbourg, 1992.

H. Donner. *Geschichte des Volkes Israel und seiner Nachbarn in Grundzügen II: Von der Königszeit bis zu Alexander dem Großen, Mit einem Ausblick auf die Geschichte des Judentums bis Bar Kochba.* 2d ed. GAT 4/2. Göttingen: Vandenhoeck & Ruprecht, 1995.

H. Stegemann. *The Library of Qumran: On the Essenes, Qumran, John the Baptist, and Jesus.* Grand Rapids: Eerdmans, 1998.

J. J. Collins. *Apocalypticism in the Dead Sea Scrolls.* New York: Routledge, 1997.

———. *Jewish Wisdom in the Hellenistic Age.* Louisville: Westminster John Knox, 1997.

J. C. VanderKam. *The Dead Sea Scrolls Today.* Grand Rapids: Eerdmans, 1994.

J. H. Hayes and S. R. Mandell. *The Jewish People in Classical Antiquity. From Alexander to Bar Kochba.* Louisville: Westminster John Knox, 1998.

2

Historical Works

1 and 2 Maccabees

Thesis: In 1 and 2 Maccabees we encounter the late biblical Jewish historiography of the Hasmonean period. It was included in the Greek but not the Hebrew Bible. In 1 Maccabees, originally written in Hebrew or Aramaic, the historiographical technique is more markedly biblical; in 2 Maccabees, composed in Greek from the outset, it is explicitly Hellenistic. While the first is unconditionally pro-Hasmonean in orientation, the more theologically reflective 2 Maccabees sees only Judas as an unquestionable hero.[1]

1 Maccabees

Thesis: First Maccabees is a pro-Hasmonean historical account that treats the period from 333, and more precisely from 175, to 135 B.C.E., that is, the

---

[1] The so-called 3 Maccabees contains an account, probably dating to the Roman period, concerning a pogrom against the Jews in the time of Ptolemy IV Philopator. Infuriated by his paralysis during the desecration of the temple in Jerusalem, he is supposed to have commanded that all Alexandrian Jews be bound and thrown before elephants. After the elephants had refused for two days to attack the Jews, and had trampled on the third day certain of the king's troops appointed to carry out the execution, the king is supposed to have changed his opinion of the Jews and organized a celebration for them on the occasion of their deliverance. See Schürer/Vermes 3.1:537–41; H. Engel, "Die Bücher der Makkabäer," in Zenger, *Einleitung,* 276. German edition: E. Kautzsch, *APAT* 1:119–35; English translation: H. Anderson, "3 Maccabees," in *OTP* 1:509–29. 4 Maccabees is a philosophical, epideictic showpiece based on the portrayal in 2 Macc 3–7 of the constant piety of the Maccabean martyrs, which hardly served a concrete purpose such as their mention in the synagogue on the memorial day for martyrs, but served to remind educated Jews in danger of assimilation of fidelity to the Torah as the source of philosophical prudence, of the power to make ethical decisions, and of overcoming passion. It was presumably written in Greek in the second half of the first century C.E. and may be the product of an educated Jew from Antioch. See Schürer/Vermes 3.1:588–93; the introduction to the German edition by H.-J. Klauck, *JSHRZ* 2.6:647–85, or to the English by H. Anderson ("4 Maccabees," in *OTP* 1:531–43).

epoch of Hellenistic reform, of religious persecution, and of the rebellion and rise of the Maccabees or Hasmoneans, from the country priest Mattathias to the death of Simon, the hereditary high priest, commander, and leader of the Jews. Originally written in Hebrew, it dates to circa 120 and certainly no later than 100 B.C.E.

Issue 1: 1 Maccabees. First Maccabees contains sixteen chapters. It consists of three parts:

1. 1:1–9 Introduction: Summary overview of the history of Alexander the Great and the disastrous rule of his successors (333–301).

2. 1:10–16:22 Body: The background and history of the Jewish rebellion led by the Maccabees and their ascent to the hereditary high priesthood up to the death of Simon (175–135).

The body consists of the following four sections:

1. 1:10–2:70   The backgrounds of the Jewish rebellion in the form of the Hellenistic reforms of the high priest Jason, the attempt by Antiochus IV to forcefully hellenize Judah, and the beginnings of the rebellion triggered by the priest Mattathias from Modein up to his death (176–167/6).

2. 3:1–9:22   Report of the battles and victories of his son Judas, nicknamed Maccabee ("the Hammer"), who, after his victories over Nicanor, Gorgias, and Lysias in December 165, cleansed and reconsecrated the temple, and after yet *another* victory over Nicanor in April 160 fell in the battle of Adasa near Jerusalem.

3. 9:23–12:53   Report of the eventful battles of Jonathan, his brother and successor, who was installed as high priest in September 150 by the alleged Seleucid king Alexander I Balas and killed in 143 by Tryphon, the vizier of Antiochus IV Epiphanes.

4. 13:1–16:22   Report of the deeds of Simon, his brother and successor, of the imprisonment and killing of Jonathan in Gilead, of Simon's recognition as independent high priest by Demetrius II in 143/2, and of his appointment as hereditary high priest by the Jews in 141, the victory of his son Jonathan over General Kendebaeus

sent by Antiochus VII Sidetes, and his subsequent murder in 135/4 by his son-in-law Ptolemaus.

3. 16:23–24 Conclusion: Reference to the annals of John Hyrcanus.

Issue 2: On the Chronology and Sources. The chronology of 1 Maccabees essentially follows the Seleucid decline that began in 312 B.C.E. (Klaus Bringmann 1983). Therefore, no conclusions can be drawn regarding various sources. On internal grounds, one may assume, nonetheless, that in addition to Jewish sources the author also had access to a Hellenistic chronicle of Seleucid rulers. Thus, Klaus-Dietrich Schunck (1954 and 1980), for example, infers from the particular affinity of the portrayal of Judas to biblical historiography and the inclusion of poetic sections the existence of a *Vita Judas* available to the author of the book.

Issue 3: The Language of and Witnesses to the Book. In contrast to 2 Maccabees, 1 Maccabees was composed in Hebrew according to the testimony of Jerome in the so-called *Prologus Galeatus* to the book of Samuel.[2] Nonetheless, it is extant only in Greek, Latin, Syriac, Arabic, and Armenian manuscripts. Because of its pro-Hasmonean, noneschatological portrayal of events, the manuscripts discovered in the caves at Qumran do not attest it.

Issue 4: Dating. The dating of the book is disputed. There is, however, agreement that, because of its pro-Roman attitude, the book must predate Pompey's conquest of Jerusalem in 63 B.C.E. Yet, dates that are more precise vary between 120 and 90 B.C.E. Thus, Klaus-Dietrich Schunck (1980) regards its author as the court chronicler of the Hasmoneans whom he dates to around 120 under John Hyrcanus (134–104) before his break with the Pharisees.[3] Contrariwise, Jonathan A. Goldstein (1976) argues with good reason for a date early in the reign of Alexander Jannaeus (103–76). He cites the following reasons: (1) the anachronism in 8:10 can only be explained if a longer period of time has passed between the events confused there, namely, the death of Judas Maccabaeus (160) and the destruction of Corinth (146); (2) the reference to the further deeds of John Hyrcanus in 16:23–24 already presumes his death; and (3) there is no reference to the inglorious situation of the Romans since the late 90s.[4] In support of this late dating, one can join Helmut Engel in referring to the pro-Hasmonean tendency of the book insofar as religious opposition to the Hasmonean

---

[2] R. Weber, ed., *Biblia Sacra: Iuxta Vulgatam Versionem* I (2d ed.; Stuttgart: Deutsche Bibelgesellschaft, 1975), 365 ll. 55–57.

[3] K.-D. Schunck, *JSHRZ* 1.4:292.

[4] J. A. Goldstein, AB 41, 62–64.

dynasty raged in this period because of its failure to separate powers between the royal and the priestly offices.[5]

Issue 5: Theological Character. First Maccabees depicts Mattathias and his sons as exemplary heroes who have done everything to restore to the temple its dignity, hitherto profaned, and to the people its freedom. In style and structure, it sketches their portrait in like fashion to the presentation of the periods of the judges and early monarchy in the Deuteronomistic History. Thereby Torah and temple piety stand in dynamic tension with political experiences and events. Judas Maccabaeus encourages the army before battles by reminding it of the earlier deliverances of the people and by calling upon it to cry out to heaven so that heaven may remember the covenant with the fathers and annihilate the overpowering army of the enemy (4:8–11).[6] As is already apparent in this brief prayer, the narrator avoids the divine name and any direct reference to God; instead he speaks of heaven (see, for example, 3:18f.; 4:10) or employs the third person masculine singular pronoun "he" (see, for example, 2:21). Prophecy is extinguished (9:27). Yet, it remains possible that a new prophet may appear in the future who will announce God's will for the treatment of the stones of the desecrated altar and for the hereditary office of high priest entrusted to Simon (4:44–46 and 14:41). Eschatological expectations are foreign to the book.

Bibliography

Introductions:
Oesterley. *Introduction,* 300–14.
Eißfeldt. *Introduction,* 576–80.
Rost. *EinlApo,* 55–58.
Schürer/Vermes 3.1, 189–96.
K.-D. Schunck, "Makkabäer, Makkabäerbücher," *TRE* 21:736–45.
J. R. Bartlett. *1 Maccabees.* Guides to Apocrypha and Pseudepigrapha; Sheffield: Sheffield Academic Press, 1998.
H. Engel. "Das Erste Makkabäerbuch," in Zenger, *Einleitung,* 275–83.

The Issues:
K.-D. Schunck. *Die Quellen des I. und II. Makkabäerbuches.* Halle: Niemeyer, 1954.

---

[5] H. Engel, "Das Erste Makkabäerbuch," in Zenger, *Einleitung,* 282.
[6] See also 1 Macc 3:18–21; 7:40–42 and similarly Jonathan in 9:44–46.

E. Bickerman. *The God of the Maccabees: Studies in the Meaning and Origin of the Maccabean Revolt.* Translated by H. R. Moehring. SJLA 32. Leiden: Brill, 1979.

M. Hengel. *Judaism and Hellenism.* Philadelphia: Fortress, 1974.

T. Fischer. *Seleukiden und Makkabäer: Beiträge zur Seleukidengeschichte und zu den politischen Ereignissen in Judäa während der 1. Hälfte des 2. Jahrhunderts v. Chr.* Bochum: Studeinverlag Brockmeyer, 1980.

————. "Heliodor im Tempel von Jerusalem: Ein hellenistischer Aspekt einer 'frommen Legende.'" Pages 122–33 in *Prophetie und geschichtliche Wirklichkeit im alten Israel: FS S. Herrmann.* Edited by R. Liwak and S. Wagner. Stuttgart: Kohlhammer, 1991.

K. Bringmann. *Hellenistische Reform und Religionsverfolgung in Judäa: Eine Untersuchung zur jüdisch-hellenistischen Geschichte (175–163 v.Chr.).* AAWG 132. Göttingen: Vandenhoeck & Ruprecht, 1983.

N. Martola. *Capture and Liberation: A Study in the Composition of the First Book of Maccabees.* AAA 63/1. Åbo: Åbo Akademi, 1984.

A. Enermalm-Ogawa. *Une langage de prière juif en grec: Le témoigne des deux premiers livres des Maccabées.* ConBNT 17. Stockholm: Almqvist & Wiksell, 1987.

J. Kampen. *The Hasedeans and the Origin of Pharisaism: A Study in 1 and 2 Maccabees.* SBLSCS 24. Atlanta: Scholars Press, 1988.

B. Bar-Kochva. *Judas Maccabaeus: The Jewish Struggle against the Seleucids.* Cambridge: Cambridge University Press, 1989.

J. Sievers. *The Hasmoneans and Their Supporters: From Mattathias to the Death of John Hyrcanus I.* Studies in the History of Judaism 6. Atlanta: Scholars Press, 1990.

Commentaries:

E. Kautzsch, *APAT,* 1900; W. O. E. Oesterley, *APOT,* 1913; H. H. Bévenot, HSAT, 1931; H. Bückers, HBK, 1939; D. Schötz, EB, 1948; A.Penna, SB, 1953; S. Tedesche and S. Zeitlin, JAL, 1954; F. M. Abel and J. Starcky, SBJ, 1961[3]; J. Bartlett, CBC, 1973; J. Goldstein, AB, 1976; K. D. Schunck, *JSHRZ,* 1980; W. Dommershausen, NEchtB, 1985; A. von Dobbeler, NSKAT, 1997; F. M. Abel, EBib, 1949; Dancy, BTT, 1954.

2 Maccabees

Thesis: Second Maccabees is based on a five-volume depiction of the background of the Jewish rebellion and the life of Judas Maccabeus by one Jason of Cyrene, a Jew who wrote in Greek. It preserves his 124 B.C.E.

epitome, the basis of the book, and an additional revision dating no later than 70 C.E. It sees in events the consequences of human guilt, divine punishment, and divine aid. With its appearances of God and angels, as well as its rhetoric, the work of Jason of Cyrene employs contemporary Greco-Hellenistic historiographic practices. In terms of the history of theology, 2 Macc 7 is particularly relevant as testimony to the growing belief in *creatio ex nihilo* as the basis of belief in the resurrection of the dead, and 12:40–45, as the first attestation of a prayer and a sacrifice for the dead.

Issue 1: Structure and Contents. Second Maccabees contains fifteen chapters arranged as follows:

1:1–2:32	*Introduction:* Festal letter and preface of the epitomist.
3:1–15:36	*Body:* Background and history of the Maccabean Rebellion up to Judas's victory over Nicanor.
15:37–39	*Conclusion:* In which the epitomist seeks the goodwill of the reader.

1:1–2:32. The book opens in 1:1–9 with a letter from the year 124/3 B.C.E. addressed by the Jews in Jerusalem and Judah to the Jews in Egypt. It announces the Hannukah festival commemorating the reconsecration of the temple. There follows in 1:10–18 a letter, supposedly written in 165 after the reconquest but before the purification and rededication of the temple, to the Jew Aristobulus, portrayed as a teacher of King Ptolemy. It also contains communication concerning the new festival. The preface of the epitomist follows in 2:19–32. In it, he informs the reader of the content and the origin of his account as his summary of the five-volume work.

3:1–15:36. The body consists of three parts:

Part A (3:1–7:42) The backgrounds of the Maccabean Rebellion.

Part B (8:1–11:38) The course of the rebellion up to Antiochus V's repeal of the religion edict.

Part C (12:1–15:36) Judas's further battles with the enemies of the Jews up to his victory over Nicanor, the general of Demetrius I.

Part A (3:1–7:42): This passage reports in 3:1–40 an initial desecration of the temple by Heliodorus, the chancellor of Seleucus IV (187–175 B.C.E.), in 4:1–50 the hellenizing reform of the high priests Jason and Menelaus, in 5:1–27 Jason's failed reconquest of Jerusalem and the plundering of the temple by Antiochus IV, and in 6:1–7:42 the prohibition and persecution of Jewish religious practices. From the perspective of the history of religions, chapter 7, with its legend of the undaunted martyrdom of the seven brothers, deserves special emphasis.

Part B (8:1–11:38): The report of Judas's deeds up to the complete restoration of religious freedom follows. It begins with the account in 8:1–33 of the beginning of the Jewish rebellion and the initial successes under Judas's leadership, successes that consisted of the defeat of the troops sent by the king under the command of Nicanor and Gorgias. The report of the defeat of the two generals, Timotheus and Bacchides, in vv. 30–33 seems to have arrived erroneously at its present position. In 9:1–9 appear a brief report concerning the campaign of Antiochus IV, then an extensive report of his death in Media, the supposed occasion of the tendentious letter to the Jews related in vv. 19–27. In it, he calls them to loyalty to his son Antiochus V, already installed as his successor.[7] In 10:1–8 are reported the cleansing and dedication of the temple, and then vv. 9–35 record Judas's further battles with General Gorgias and, presumably, also with the commander Timotheus. Judas's troops surrounded him in a castle named Gazara (Gezer) on the coast and, after conquering it, killed him. According to 11:1–15, the guardian of the young King Lysias marched against Judah with a strong force, yet Judas defeated him near Jerusalem, so that he recognized his error and sought peace on equitable terms. As evidence, the record of four original documents follows, the first stemming from Lysias, the second from Antiochus V, the third from Antiochus IV, and the fourth from the Roman legates Quintus Mummius and Titus Manius.

Part C (12:1–15:36): Here Judas's victories over the local Seleucid commanders between Joppa (Jaffa) and Skythopolis (Beth Shean) are first reported along with those over the governor of Idumea in the wilderness of Judah (11:2–45). In addition, the account in 12:40–45 of the burial of the fallen Jewish idolaters contains the oldest attestation of faith in the efficacy of intercession and atonement for the dead. A report follows in 13:1–26 concerning (1) the intended occupation of Judah by Antiochus V; (2) the execution, on his command, of the high priest Menelaus (vv. 3–8); (3) the alleged intention of the Seleucid king to retract the concession made to the Jews (vv. 9–11); (4) Judas's operations, which forced the king to undertake raids that ceased on Antiochus's sudden withdrawal at news of the mental illness of the imperial administrator, Philip; and (5) the peace pact with the Jews. Then 14:1–15:36 reports that Alcimus, the new

---

[7] Regarding evidence of inauthenticity, see C. Habicht, *JSHRZ* 1.6:246 n.18a; but see also J. Goldstein, AB 41A, 357–58, who does not want to rule out the possibility that the letter represents a counterfeit fashioned by Lysias.

high priest who had meanwhile fled the country, convinced Demetrius I Soter (162–150), the successor of Antiochus V, to send Nicanor with an elephant corps to Judah. There he graciously received Judas in Jerusalem until Alcimus poisoned Nicanor against him. Only then did it come to a decisive battle near Samaria in which Judas prevailed and Nicanor fell. The exemplary account of the death of a certain Razis, "father of the Jews," is interwoven into this report in 14:37–46.

Issue 2: The Book and Its Sources. In its preface, the book describes itself as an excerpt from a five-volume history of Judas Maccabaeus by *Jason of Cyrene*, who may have been a contemporary of the events. Yet, it may well have also referred to Eupolemus's history of the Jews that reached to the year 158 B.C.E. (see 4:11).[8] Of the two letters in 1:1–2:18 prefixed subsequently, the first is authentic,[9] the second a counterfeit[10] (as is the letter of Antiochus IV in 9:19–27). On the other hand, all four of the letters transmitted in 11:16–37 are authentic documents, although incorrectly interpreted by the context and, in part, incorrectly sequenced chronologically.

Probable post-Jason edifying insertions are (1) the temple scene in the Heliodorus account in 3:24–33; (2) the interpretative note in 4:17; (3) the expansions of the accounts of the punitive expedition of Antiochus IV against Judea in 5:17–20 and of the martyrdom of Eleazar in 6:18–17; (4) the legend of the martyrdom of the seven brothers in 7:1–41; (5) the letter of Antiochus IV in 9:18–27; and probably also (6) the references to the doctrine of the resurrection in 12:43–45 and 14:37–46 and (7) the comment concerning the inauguration in 15:36 of Nicanor Day as a holiday one day before Mordecai Day.[11] In addition, the epitomist strengthened the theological and moral accents and introduced outright the eschatologically oriented sections.[12] Finally, the Seleucid dating that begins with the spring of 312 notably underlies the chronological information in 2 Maccabees, as well as in 1 Maccabees.[13]

Issue 3: The Date and the Author. The work of Jason of Cyrene must date from between 160 and 124; yet, it is likely that he had already completed

---

[8] See also N. Walter, *Fragmente jüdisch-hellenistischer Historiker* (*JSHRZ* 1.2; Gütersloh: Mohn, 1980), 93.

[9] See E. Bickerman, "Ein jüdischer Festbrief vom Jahre 124 v.Chr.," *ZNW* 32 (1933): 233–54 (= *Studies in Jewish and Christian History II* [Leiden: Brill, 1980], 136–58).

[10] On the discussion, see J. Goldstein, *I Maccabees*, 157–63, who dates it to the year 103/2 when both the Oniads and Alexander Jannaeus found themselves in distress.

[11] That is, Purim; see Esth 9:17–19.

[12] See also the overview in K.-D. Schunck, "Makkabäer, Makkabäerbücher," *TRE* 21: 739.

[13] See Bringmann, *Hellenistische Reform*, 16–27, esp. 27.

his work a few years after Judas's death. On the assumption that the letter in 1:1–8 and the epitomist's preface in 2:19–32*[14] stem from the same year, the basic draft of the book belongs to the year 124. The expansions produced in connection with the incorporation of the letter in 1:10–2:18 were undertaken in any case after 124 B.C.E. and before the destruction of the temple in 70 C.E., probably in the first century C.E. His theological attitude indicates a connection between the epitomist and eschatologically-oriented Jewish circles.

Issue 4: Literary and Historico-theological Character. Judging from its literary character, the book is testimony to Hellenistic Judaism—for if its piety is Jewish, its historiographic approach is Greek. In contrast to 1 Maccabees, events fall here under the rubrics of guilt and atonement, penalty and grace. Accordingly, the book reports the inner-Jewish background for Antiochus IV's religious persecution more extensively than does 1 Maccabees. Yet, God not only acts indirectly by guiding the course of history, but he also appears directly from heaven at decisive moments or has other heavenly beings intervene in events.[15] Whereas one can characterize 1 Maccabees as unequivocally pro-Hasmonean, 2 Maccabees adopts a cool to critical stance toward the Hasmoneans, with the exception of Judas (see, for example, 10:19–20 and 14:17).[16] In its historiographical technique, it participates in the lofty style of contemporary Hellenistic rhetorical historiography with its preference for signs and wonders, its demonstration of the horrific end of evildoers, and not least its joy in the appearance of gods such as Apollo or Heracles at decisive moments (of course for the Jewish author God or God's angels take the field).[17] For effect the epitomist would set aside the historical sequence of events. In doubtful cases, therefore, the historian will adhere to the sequence in 1 Maccabees.[18]

Comment 1: The Letters in 11:1–37. Four documents are transmitted here: a communication of Chancellor Lysias to the Jews, a letter of Antiochus V to Lysias, a communication of Antiochus IV to the Jews, erroneously placed in third position, and, finally, a letter of two Roman legates, again to the Jews. In proper sequence, they contain indispensable information concerning the end of religious persecution of the Jews. According to

---

[14] The asterisk marks a text that is not a primary literary unit, but one enlarged by secondary additions.

[15] See, for example, 2:21; 12:22; 3:24–30; 10:29–31; and 12:22.

[16] See Habicht, *JSHRZ* 1.6, 188.

[17] See Habicht, *JSHRZ* 1.6, 190.

[18] See also Bringmann, *Hellenistische Reform*, 36–38 and 52–56.

Klaus Bringmann, the letters are to be arranged and dated as follows.[19] In first position temporally and in literary sequence stands the September/ October 165 letter of Chancellor Lysias to the Jews. In it, he alludes to his past dealings with the Jews in which he conceded to them that over which he had authority, while on the other points he awaited the royal decision. There follows temporally the letter of Antiochus IV to the Jews, occupying third position in vv. 27–33, which, contrary to its dating,[20] stems from November/December 165 and promises the Jews amnesty should they return home prior to May 164. Chronologically linked to it is sequentially the final (vv. 33–38) document, that of the Roman legates Q. Mummius and T. Manius to the Jewish people. In it, they take a stance on the Jews' ongoing dealings with Lysias. The undated letter of Antiochus V Eupator, standing in second position in vv. 22–26, also addresses Lysias. It announces the change of sovereign and guarantees the Jews the legal restitution of the temple and return to their ancestral way of life. It may have been composed around the turn of the year 164/163.

Comment 2: The Significance of Chapter 7. The seventh chapter holds particular interest for the historian of religion as well as for theologians because it grounds the future resurrection of the dead in the statement that God did not make heaven and earth and everything that fills it from preexistent materials (see also Rom 4:17). Therefore, it involves both an early witness to the concept of the bodily resurrection of the pious as well as a precursor to the doctrine of creation from nothing, *creatio ex nihilo.*[21]

Comment 3: Transmission of the Text. The transmission of the text of the book, written in Greek from the outset, encompasses the two uncial manuscripts Alexandrinus and Venetus as well as a large number of Greek minuscule manuscripts. Additionally, there are a number of manuscripts of Latin, Syriac, and Armenian translations, as well as one fragment of a Coptic version. Robert Hanhart based the standard edition of the Greek text (1959) primarily on Alexandrinus and the minuscules 55, 347, and 771.[22]

---

[19] Bringmann, *Hellenistische Reform,* 40–51.

[20] Contrary to the date, identical with v. 38, of the Roman document. Habicht, *JSHRZ* 1.6, 179–85, assigned the sequence 3, 1, 4, and 2, dating all these documents except number 2 to the time of Antiochus IV.

[21] See G. May, *Schöpfung aus dem Nichts: Die Entstehung der Lehre von der* creatio ex nihilo (AKG 48; New York: de Gruyter, 1978), 1–40.

[22] For a review, see Habicht, *JSHRZ* 1.6, 192–93, and his list of preferred variants (384–85).

Bibliography

Introductions:
Oesterley. *Introduction*, 315–25.
Eißfeldt. *Introduction*, 576–80.
Rost. *EinlApo*, 58–61.
Schürer/Vermes 3.1, 531–37.
K.-D. Schunck. "Makkabäer/Makkabäerbücher," *TRE* 21:739–45.
H. Engel, "Das Zweite Makkabäerbuch," in Zenger, *Einleitung*, 283–90.

The Text:
R. Hanhart, *Maccabaeorum liber II copiis usus quas reliquit Werner Kappler.*
2d ed. Septuaginta IX/2. Göttingen: Vandenhoeck & Ruprecht, 1976.
———. "Zum Text des 2. und 3. Makkabäerbuches. Probleme der Überlieferung, der Auslegung und der Ausgabe." NAWG (1961): 427–86.

Discussion:
B. Niese. "Kritik der beiden Makkabäerbücher nebst Beiträgen zur Ge-
schichte der makkabäischen Erhebung." *Hermes* 35 (1900): 268–307,
453–527.
J. Wellhausen. "Über den geschichtlichen Wert des zweiten Makkabäer-
buches im Verhältnis zum ersten." NGWG 2 (1905): 117–63.
E. Bickerman. "Ein jüdischer Festbrief vom Jahre 124 v.Chr." *ZNW* 32
(1933): 233–54 (= Pages 136–58 in E. Bickerman. *Studies in Jewish and
Christian History II.* Leiden: Brill, 1980).
W. Surkau. *Martyrien in jüdischer und frühchristlicher Zeit.* FRLANT 54.
Göttingen: Vandenhoeck & Ruprecht, 1938.
M. Hengel. *Judaism and Hellenism.* Philadelphia: Fortress, 1974.
J. G. Bunge. "Untersuchungen zum zweiten Makkabäerbuch." PhD diss.,
Bonn University, 1971.
G. May. *Schöpfung aus dem Nichts: Die Entstehung der Lehre von der* creatio
ex nihilo. AKG 48. New York: de Gruyter, 1978.
B. Z. Wacholder. "The Letter from Judah Maccabee to Aristobulus: Is
2 Maccabees 1:10b–2:18 Authentic?" *HUCA* 49 (1978): 89–133.
R. Doran. *Temple Propaganda: The Purpose and Character of 2 Maccabees.*
CBQMS 12. Washington, D.C.: Catholic Biblical Association of Amer-
ica, 1981.

Commentaries:
A. Kamphausen *APAT,* 1900; J. Moffatt, *APOT,* 1913; H. Bévenot, HSAT,
1931; H. Bückers, HBK, 1939; A. Penna, SB, 1953; S. Tedesche and Zeitlin,
JAL, 1954; E. M. Abel and J. Starcky, SBJ, 1961³; J. Bartlett, CBC, 1973;

C. Habicht, *JSHRZ*, 1976 (1979²); J. Goldstein, AB, 1983; W. Dommershausen, NEchtB, 1986; A. von Dobbeler, NSKAT, 1997.

3 Ezra

Thesis: The Hebrew Bible does not attest the document designated variously 3 Ezra in the Vulgate and Esdras in the Septuagint. The Septuagint transmits the oldest state of its text. The document contains nine chapters, beginning with the report of Josiah's Passover celebration and ending with Ezra's public reading of the Torah. Because of the seamless transition between its account of the dissolution of the mixed marriages in 8:69–9:36 and the list of returnees and the account of Ezra's public reading of the Torah in 9:37–55, which corresponds to the sequence of events in Ezra 9:1–10:44 and Neh 7:72–8:13a, some research understandably concluded that 3 Ezra is an older edition of the Chronistic History that did not yet include the book of Nehemiah. Its chief distinctive feature consists in the account of the contest of the three pages at the court of King Darius in 3:1–5:6.

Comment 1: The Divergent Enumeration and Transmission of the Books of Ezra in the Hebrew Bible, the Septuagint, the Vulgate, and the NRSV.

Modern MT		LXX	Vulgate	NRSV
1 Ezra	Ezra	2 Esdras (β)	1 Esdras	Ezra
2 Ezra	Nehemiah	2 Esdras (γ)	2 Esdras	Nehemiah
3 Ezra	———	1 Esdras (α)	3 Esdras	1 Esdras
4 Ezra	———	———	4 Esdras 3–14	2 Esdras 3–14
5 Ezra	———	———	4 Esdras 1–2	2 Esdras 1–2
6 Ezra	———	———	4 Esdras 15–16	2 Esdras 15–16

Comment 2: The Parallels Between 3 Ezra and Chronicles/Ezra/Nehemiah:[23]

3 Ezra 1:1–20	= 2 Chr 35:1–19
3 Ezra 1:21–22	no parallel
3 Ezra 1:23–55	= 2 Chr 35:20–36:21
3 Ezra 2:1–5a	= 2 Chr 36:22–23 = Ezra 1:1–3a

---

[23] According to S. Mowinckel, *Studien zu dem Buche Ezra-Nehemia I: Die nachchronistische Redaktion des Buches: Die Listen* (SNVAO NS 3; Oslo: Universitetsforlaget, 1964), 12; K.-F. Pohlmann, *Studien zum dritten Esra: Ein Beitrag zur Frage nach dem ursprünglichen Schluß des chronistischen Geschichtswerks* (FRLANT 104; Göttingen: Vandenhoeck & Ruprecht, 1970), 14; K.-F. Pohlmann, *JSHRZ* 1.5:377.

3 Ezra 2:5b–14	= Ezra 1:3b–11
3 Ezra 2:15–25	= Ezra 4:7–24
3 Ezra 3:1–5:6	no parallel
3 Ezra 5:7–70	= Ezra 2:1–4:5
3 Ezra 6:1–9:36	= Ezra 5:1–10:44
3 Ezra 9:37–55	= Neh 7:72–8:13a.

Comment 3: The Character of the Translation. The Greek translation of 3 Ezra was produced directly from the Hebrew or, in 2:15–25, from the Aramaic.[24] It leaves a mixed impression. On the one hand, it translates more adroitly and freely than Esdras β and γ, and on the other, it does not render the central theological concepts with terminological consistency as is the case in the two other books. Consequently, some researchers judge it to be older, the majority younger.[25] Nevertheless, analysis of the content supports the first view. The divergent diction and the terminological fusion at its boundaries betray the narrative of the pages in 3 Ezra as originally independent literarily.[26] It presumably derives from an Aramaic original.[27]

Issue 1: The Grounds Forwarded for the Priority of 3 Ezra.[28] Gustav Hölscher,[29] Sigmund Mowinckel,[30] and Karl-Friedrich Pohlmann[31] have pointed out that in 3 Ezra, Neh 7:72–8:13a follows immediately on Ezra 10 and that the Jewish historian Flavius Josephus, who apparently utilized 3 Ezra,[32] has Ezra die before Nehemiah's arrival in Jerusalem (*Ant.* 11). Accordingly, Josephus must have had before him an Ezra text in which the Ezra account was not yet linked to the Nehemiah account.[33] Therefore, they concluded that 3 Ezra constitutes the end of an older edition of the Chronistic History. Assuming the accuracy of this reconstruction, it follows that the celebration of a festival on every positive event in Israel's history characterizes the Chronistic portrayal. Consequently, the Festival

---

[24] Mowinckel, *Ezra-Nehemia I*, 7–12.

[25] See Pohlmann, *JSHRZ* 1.5, 378–79.

[26] See Pohlmann, *Studien*, 50–51 and 150–51; Pohlmann, *JSHRZ* 1.5, 381.

[27] See Pohlmann, *Studien*, 48–49; Pohlmann, *JSHRZ* 1.5, 382.

[28] For a review of research from J. D. Michaelis to S. Mowinckel, see Pohlmann, *Studien*, 19–26.

[29] G. Hölscher, HSAT 2:495–96.

[30] Mowinckel, *Ezra-Nehemia I*, 12–28.

[31] Pohlmann, *Studien*, 53–73 and 76–114; compare Pohlmann, *JSHRZ* 1.5, 383–85.

[32] See the comparative lists in Pohlmann, *Studien*, 76–114.

[33] See also the discussion of *Ant.* 11:154ff. and 3 Ezra 9:37–55 by A. van der Kooij, "On the Ending of the Book of 1 Esdras," in *VII Congress of the International Organization for Septuagint and Cognate Studies: Leuven 1989* (ed. C. E. Cox et al.; SBLSCS 31; Atlanta: Scholars Press, 1991), 37–49.

of Booths after the construction of the temple and after the reforms of Hezekiah and Josiah, Passover after the return from exile, and once again the Festival of Booths after the dissolution of mixed marriages mark the caesurae in Israel's history.[34]

This hypothesis, often disputed over the course of the last two decades, has been confirmed by a precise comparison of the texts of Zipora Talshir[35], and raised to a certainty by the subsequent investigations of Dieter Böhler[36] and Lester L. Grabbe[37] involving comparisons of the content of the two parallel texts, 3 Ezra 2; 5:7–9:55 and Ezra 1–10 and Neh 8–12. Böhler was able to show that the book of Ezra secondarily transformed Jerusalem into a heap of ruins,[38] partially rearranged the Artaxerxes correspondence, and limited its significance to the construction of the temple.[39] Consequently, the construction of the altar, which appears after the correspondence in 3 Ezra, has also been shifted to the fore.[40] In this manner, the editor responsible for the Hebrew Ezra prepares for the Nehemiah account.[41] Böhler places this redactional activity in the time of the Maccabeean war of liberation.[42] Correspondingly, Grabbe emphasizes that the biblical Ezra-Nehemiah narrative consists of two foundation legends. The book of Ezra with its concentration on the temple represents one, and the book of Nehemiah with its concentration on the reconstruction of the city walls, the other. Thus, he concludes that 3 Ezra offers the older portrayal. By no means do the two investigations have interest merely for the history of literature; rather, they bear consequences for the reconstruction of Israel's history in the Persian period. According to the judgment of both, the historian should rely on 3 Ezra rather than Ezra.

---

[34] Pohlmann, *Studien*, 127–43.

[35] Z. Talshir, "Double Translations in the Septuagint," in *VIth Congress of the International Organization of Septuagint and Cognate Studies: Jerusalem 1980* (ed. C. E. Cox; SBLSCS 23; Atlanta: Scholars Press, 1986), 21–63.

[36] D. Böhler, *Die heilige Stadt in Esdras und Esra-Nehemia: Zwei Konzepte der Wiederherstellung Israels* (OBO 158; Göttingen: Vandenhoeck & Ruprecht, 1997).

[37] L. L. Grabbe, *Ezra and Nehemiah* (Readings; New York: Routledge, 1998).

[38] Böhler, *Heilige Staat*, 144–79.

[39] Böhler, *Heilige Staat*, 216–65.

[40] Compare 3 Ezra 5:46–70 with Ezra 3:1–4:5.

[41] J. Becker, *Der Ich-Bericht des Nehemiabuches als chronistische Gestaltung* (FB 87; Würzburg: Echter, 1998), disputes the existence of a Nehemiah memoir and judges the account to be Chronistic; see already Becker, *Esra/Nehemia* (NEchtB; Würzburg: Echter, 1990), 6. He expresses himself, however, against the earlier date of 3 Ezra. He puts the Chronistic History after 400 and probably later than 300.

[42] Böhler, *Heilige Staat*, 382–97. Only Ezra 8:16 and Neh 11:10, 21–24; 12:1–26 give consideration retrospectively to the Hasmonean dynasty. Conversely, M. Carrez ("1. Esdras Septante," *RHPR* 74 [1994]: 13–42) dates 3 Ezra to circa 150 B.C.E. and locates it in Alexandria.

Issue 2: The Reasons Forwarded for the Notion that 3 Ezra Is a Secondary Compilation. As a rule, a compilation hypothesis has been offered to explain the origin of 3 Ezra.[43] According to this view, the book represents a secondary excerpt from the Chronistic History, which already contained the book of Nehemiah, or from 2 Chronicles and Ezra-Nehemiah. Thus, for example, Wilhelm Rudolph declares the sequence of events in the biblical book of Ezra to be internally more consistent,[44] and the better style of 3 Ezra to be the result of its later origins in relation to the Septuagint translation (an argument susceptible to varied assessments).[45] His chief objection, that the story of the pages was already an original component of 3 Ezra,[46] has been refuted by Pohlmann.[47] H. G. M. Williamson's objection against the fragment hypothesis,[48] which he offered in connection with his refutation of the existence of a Chronistic History, has made a particular impression. For him, the use of 2 Chr 33:9 in 3 Ezra 1:22 represents an argument that the translation of 3 Ezra began before Manasseh's reign. In the ultimate question for the evaluation of the source, whether 3 Ezra 9:37 knows the relationship between Neh 7:72a and 8:1 and thus the combination of the Ezra narrative with that of Nehemiah, he votes for the retention of the transmitted wording. The divergent treatment of the parallels Ezra 2:7 and 3:1 in 3 Ezra 5:45–46 is no indication of another exemplar, in his eyes; rather, it corresponds to 3 Ezra's free handling of its exemplar observable elsewhere.[49] Williamson finds an additional argument in favor of the traditional compilation hypothesis in the fact that, while Ezra 2 depends upon Neh 7:3, in his view, Ezra 5:7–45 depends upon Ezra 2.[50]

Comment 4: The Story of the Pages, 3:1–5:6. This account reports the contest of the three Jewish pages at the court of Darius. When, after a meal he had given for all his servants and the magnates of the realm, Darius had fallen fitfully asleep on his bed, each of his three bodyguards wrote in one

---

[43] See recently G. Steins, "Die Bücher Esra und Nehemia," in Zenger, *Einleitung,* 239, who leans toward the traditional solution, but considers the question to remain open.

[44] W. Rudolph, HAT, 1.20, xiv–xvi.

[45] Rudolph, HAT, 1.20, xvi.

[46] Rudolph, HAT, 1.20, xvii.

[47] Pohlmann, *Studien,* 50–51 and 150–51; Pohlmann, *JSHRZ* 1.5, 378–79.

[48] H. G. M. Williamson, *Israel in the Book of Chronicles* (New York: Cambridge University Press, 1977). See my review in Zenger, *Einleitung,* 192–94.

[49] See Williamson, *Israel in the Book of Chronicles,* 29–34 and the conclusion, 35–36. He does not dispute the fact that Josephus based his portrait on 3 Ezra and began anew with his portrait of Nehemiah, but he sees in it no evidence for the primary literary relationship of the Ezra narrative with Chronicles (21–29).

[50] H. G. M. Williamson, "The Problem with First Esdras," in *Guides to Apocrypha and Pseudepigrapha* (ed. Barton et al.; Macon: Mercer, 1996), 201–16.

word what they considered to be the mightiest thing on earth and placed the sealed slip of paper under the king's pillow. When Darius had awakened and read the notes, he invited the leading figures of the realm once again in order to have each of the youths justify his choice. The first explained why wine, the second why the king, and the third why women are the mightiest on this earth. The third youth, who was none other than Zerubbabel, succeeded in showing that all men, including the king, no matter whether mighty or insignificant, would sacrifice everything for the sake of love for a woman. Thereupon, Darius awarded Zerubbabel the prize of wishing for whatever he wanted. He reminded the king, however, of his vow to send back the instruments carried away from the Jerusalem temple to Babylon and to permit the reconstruction of the temple, which the king then immediately granted along with additional decrees in favor of the temple cult and the Jews. This paraphrase may have already demonstrated that the identification of the third page with Zerubbabel occurred secondarily and that, accordingly, the entire conclusion relating to the restitution of the Jerusalem temple is the product of a revision that presumably traces back to the interpolator who inserted it into 3 Ezra.[51]

Bibliography

Introduction:
Oesterley. *Introduction,* 133–41.
Eißfeldt. *Introduction,* 574–76.
Rost. *EinlApo,* 71–73.
Schürer/Vermes 3.2, 708–18.
G. Steins. "Die Bücher Esra und Nehemia," in Zenger, *Einleitung,* 239.

Issues:
S. Mowinckel. *Studien zu dem Buche Ezra-Nehemia I: Die nachchronistische Redaktion des Buches: Die Listen.* SNVAO NS 3. Oslo: Universitetsforlaget, 1964.
———. *Studien zu dem Buche Ezra-Nehemia II: Die Nehemia-Denkschrift.* SNVAO NS 5. Oslo: Universitetsforlaget, 1964.

---

[51] Concerning the multiphased background of the story, the core of which is not primarily Jewish, see the extensive treatment in Pohlmann, *Studien,* 35–47, or the brief treatment in Pohlmann, *JSHRZ* 1.5, 380–83. On the Persian background of the question concerning truth, see A. Hilhorst, "The Speech of Truth in 1 Esdras 4,34–41," in *The Scriptures and the Scrolls: Studies in Honour of A. S. van der Woude on the Occasion of His 65th Birthday* (ed. F. García Martínez; VTSup 49; Leiden: Brill, 1992), 135–51.

————. *Studien zu dem Buche Ezra-Nehemia III: Die Ezrageschichte und das Gesetz des Moses.* SNVAO NS 7. Oslo: Universitetsforlaget, 1965.

K.-F. Pohlmann. *Studien zum dritten Esra: Ein Beitrag zur Frage nach dem ursprünglichen Schluß des chronistischen Geschichtswerks.* FRLANT 104. Göttingen: Vandenhoeck & Ruprecht, 1970.

H. G. M. Williamson. *Israel in the Book of Chronicles.* New York: Cambridge University Press, 1977.

————. "The Problem with First Esdras." Pages 201–16 in *Guides to Apocrypha and Pseudepigrapha.* Edited by J. Barton et al. Macon: Mercer, 1996.

T. Muraoka. *A Greek-Hebrew-Aramaic Index to I Esdras.* SBLSCS 16. Chico: Scholars Press, 1984.

Z. Talshir. "Double Translations in the Septuagint." Pages 21–63 in *VIth Congress of the International Organization of Septuagint and Cognate Studies: Jerusalem 1980.* Edited by C. E. Cox. SBLSCS 23. Atlanta: Scholars Press, 1986.

A. van der Kooij. "On the Ending of the Book of 1 Esdras." Pages 37–49 in *VII Congress of the International Organization for Septuagint and Cognate Studies: Leuven 1989.* Edited by C. E. Cox et al. SBLSCS 31. Atlanta: Scholars Press, 1991.

A. Hilhorst. "The Speech of Truth in 1 Esdras 4,34–41." Pages 135–51 in *The Scriptures and the Scrolls: Studies in Honour of A. S. van der Woude on the Occasion of His 65th Birthday.* Edited by F. García Martínez. VTSup 49. Leiden: Brill, 1992.

M. Carrez. "1. Esdras Septante." *RHPR* 74 (1994): 13–42.

D. Böhler. *Die heilige Stadt in Esdras und Esra-Nehemia: Zwei Konzepte der Wiederherstellung Israels.* OBO 158. Göttingen: Vandenhoeck & Ruprecht, 1997.

L. L. Grabbe. *Ezra and Nehemia.* Readings. New York: Routledge, 1998.

Commentaries:

H. Guthe, *APAT,* 1900; S. A. Cook, *APOT,* 1913; G. Hölscher, HSAT II[4] 1923; W. Rudolph, HAT, 1955; R.-F. Pohlmann, *JSHRZ,* 1980.

3

Deuterocanonical Narratives

The Book of Tobit

Thesis 1: In terms of its literary character, the book of Tobit is a didactic narrative with novelistic features based on fairy tale and biblical motifs. As such, it is evidence of Jewish narrative art and piety from the early Hellenistic period. It deals with the piety and the suffering of the Naphtalite Tobit whom Shalmaneser had taken to Nineveh, and above all with the successful journey of his son Tobias. Sent by his father to call in a loan once guaranteed him, he brings not only the silver, thanks to the guidance of the archangel Raphael, but also salve for his father's eyes, and for himself a pious wife in the figure of his relative Sarah. Thus, the book of Tobit attests a piety shaped by prayer and good works, a piety that includes the idea that the angels bring the prayers of the pious before God and guide them on their way.

Issue 1: The Structure of the Book. Apart from the superscription in 1:1–2, the book of Tobit divides into three parts: (1) the *Introduction* (1:3–3:17, framework narrative I with a dual exposition), (a) Tobit's first-person report of his fate and his prayer to die (1:3–36), and (b) a third-person report concerning the pious Sarah and her prayer to die (3:7–15), held together by the report that God hears their prayers and sends Raphael (3:16–17); (2) the *Body* with the internal plot in the form of the account of the successful journey and return of Tobit's son Tobias with his wife Sarah, under the guidance of the angel (4:1–12:22 [13:1–14:1]); and (3) the *Conclusion* (framework narrative II) with the report of Tobit's testament and his and his son's deaths (14:2–15).

Issue 2: The Genre of the Book.[1] The book of Tobit contains fairy tale motifs but is no fairy tale. Based on its content, it may more readily be

---

[1] See the extensive discussion by P. Deselaers, *Das Buch Tobit: Studien zu seiner Entstehung, Komposition und Theologie* (OBO 43; Göttingen: Vandenhoeck & Ruprecht, 1982), 261–79.

characterized as a wisdom moral tale with didactic tendencies, although this does not sufficiently describe its literary form. In accordance with its scope, stretching from the father's loss of sight to his healing, one could more easily characterize it as a novella. Yet, both the grounding of the story in the context of world history and the multiple plot lines already foreshadowed in the introduction indicate a novel, for which the open narrative form is characteristic. Thus, one can best describe the book as a wisdom moral tale with novelistic features.[2]

Comment 1: The Content of the Book.[3] The content of the book may be summarized as follows: Tobit, the son of Tobiel from the tribe of Naphtali, who was deported to Nineveh in the days of the Assyrian king Shalmaneser, reports that, together with his wife Hannah and his son Tobias, he consistently lived in precise observance of the cultic and dietary prescriptions of the law and was particularly careful to clothe the naked[4] and to bury his compatriots slain by the Assyrian king Sennacherib. Though a royal purchasing agent under Shalmaneser, under his successor Sennacherib Tobit had been banished and his possessions confiscated. Only after Sennacherib's death was he able to return to Nineveh on the intercession of his nephew Ahiqar, who had risen to be Esarhaddon's chief accountant. But now a new misfortune has overtaken him; for when he was burying a member of his people found strangled by his son in the marketplace during the weekly festival, sparrow excrement fell into both his eyes so that when even his wife reviled him, he begged God to let him die (1:2–3:6). At the same time, the young Jewess Sarah, the daughter of Raguel who lived in Ecbatana in Media, also prayed for death or deliverance, for she had lost seven husbands on her wedding nights so that her maidens accused her of murder (3:7–15). Then God heard both prayers in the presence of Raphael whom he sent to heal Tobit and to bind the demon Ashmodeaus who was killing Sarah's suitors (3:16–17).

In his poverty and sorrow, however, Tobit remembered that he had once given ten silver talents for safekeeping to a fellow Naphtalite named Gabael in Rages in Media. Consequently, he decided to send Tobias there to reclaim his property. Since he reckoned on his own death, Tobit admonished his departing son to bury him on his return, and later his mother, too, and to continue to live in a manner pleasing to God (4:1–21). Tobias

---

[2] See also C. A. Moore, AB 40A, 17–21, who proposes designating it a novel; and B. Ego, *JSHRZ* 2.6, 884, who proposes a wisdom moral tale.

[3] See also the structural outline in H. Engel, "Das Buch Tobit," in Zenger, *Einleitung,* 248–49.

[4] Compare Isa 58:7.

obeyed willingly and set out—to the sorrow of his mother Hannah, who was comforted by Tobit—on his journey along with his dog and his companion Azariah, hired in the marketplace, who claimed to be the son of the great Ananias, but who was in truth none other than the archangel Raphael (5:1–6:1a). As Tobias bathed in the Tigris on the evening of the first day of travel, a great fish attacked him.[5] At the bidding of his companion, he courageously seized and killed the fish and removed its heart, liver, and gallbladder to preserve as a remedy. Heart and liver were to serve as incense for expelling a demon that had entered a person, and the gallbladder for healing white spots on the eyes (that is, cataracts; 6:1b–9). Before they came to Ecbatana, Azariah informed Tobias that they would lodge there with Raguel, whose only child, his daughter Sarah, was fated to be his wife. Azariah also told him that since he now had in his possession the means to expel the demon who had to that point been killing her husbands, he need not fear marrying her (6:10–18). Everything occurred as Azariah had predicted. Raguel and his wife Edna identified Tobias as the son of a relative,[6] and Azariah successfully asked Raguel on his behalf for Sarah's hand (7:1–17). It was possible to solemnize the marriage of the two immediately the following evening because the incense with fish's heart and liver had expelled the demon (8:1–9). Then, following the appropriate thanksgiving, the wedding was celebrated festively for fourteen days (8:19–21). Thereafter, at Tobias's request, Raphael and four servants retrieved the silver from Gabel in Rages (9:1–6). Meanwhile, Tobias's parents worried about their son's delay (10:1–7a). He took his leave, however, from Raguel and Edna after the end of the wedding celebration and set out with Sarah and Azariah for home, full of thankfulness to God. Since Sarah received half of her parents' possessions, an entire caravan followed them (10:7b–13).

When they were near Nineveh, Tobias (and his dog) went on ahead of everyone to his parents, healed his father's blindness by means of the fish's gallbladder, and told them that he had married Sarah and that she waited at the city gate (11:1–15). Then Tobit joyously received Sarah and held an additional wedding celebration (11:16–18). Afterward, father and son agreed to reward the faithful Azariah with half of that which Tobias had brought from his journey (12:1–5), but Azariah admonished them to praise God and reminded them that the prayers of the merciful are heard and good works are rewarded with a long life. Then he revealed himself as Raphael, one of the seven angels who stand in the presence of God's

---

[5] His cry of distress, "Help, Lord, it wants to devour me!" which became a familiar saying, apparently represents a later interpretation, since it appears only in the Vulgate and thus also in Luther's Bible.

[6] G I: of a brother, G II: of a cousin.

majesty, and disappeared from their sight while they praised and lauded God (12:6–22). Tobit 13:1–18 then follows with Tobit's song of thanksgiving admonishing Israel to be thankful for God's saving acts in its first section (vv. 1b–8) and promising it God's renewed attention should they repent. The second section (vv. 9–18) follows with an eschatological song of praise for Jerusalem. Then follows (14:1–11) the report of Tobit's age, his last words to Tobias, and his death and burial. In his last words, the dying man showed himself to be a prophet, whose vision encompassed history up to the time of the future glorification of Jerusalem following its destruction. Therefore, he advised his son to leave Nineveh with his seven sons before the imminent destruction of the city and to reach safety in Media. Thus Tobit and his family moved to Ecbatana where he buried his mother, inherited Raguel's estate along with his father's, and died at the age of 117 after he had received the news of the fall of Nineveh (14:13–15).

Issue 3: Tradition and Motif History. Disregarding the numerous biblical allusions,[7] whose secondary nature we have already mentioned, the fairy tale of the bride of the monster distinguishes itself as the central motif of the narrative. The form most closely related to the Tobit account is present in an Armenian fairy tale of the grateful deceased in which the spirit of the deceased, in gratitude for his burial by the hero, kills the demon who intends to kill him on his wedding night. Thus Sven Liljeblad proposes the possibility that the fairy tale and the Tobit account have influenced one another. Decisive for understanding the book of Tobit, however, is the way the fairy tale is transformed and integrated into Yahwism (Paul Deselaers). The intervention of the deliverer is now the consequence of prayer heeded by Yahweh, and the aiding spirit has become an angel from Yahweh's court, who, carrying out the promise of Gen 24:7, accompanies Tobias on his journey to his bride. This transformation need not be the work of the author of the book of Tobit; it could be based on a narrative current among his contemporaries that, according to Lothar Ruppert (1972), told of the travel experiences of Tobit the merchant. Additionally, the merchant would have become the father blinded by his piety who sends his son on journeys. Simultaneously, the bride Sarah would also have been assigned her own role in the exposition. Thus, the narrative developed a complex storyline and, at the same time, became more significant for its Diaspora context.

Issue 4: Text and Original Language. The book of Tobit is represented by five fragmentary manuscripts from Cave 4 at Qumran—four Aramaic and

---

[7] Regarding dependence on the ancestral narratives, see M. Rabenau, *Studien zum Buch Tobit* (BZAW 220; New York: de Gruyter, 1994); and Moore, AB 40A, 8–9.

one Hebrew (4Q196–200)—which account for 20 percent of the Aramaic and 4 percent of the Hebrew text.[8] They stem from the time between 100 B.C.E. and 50 C.E. and attest to bilinguality in Palestine in the last century B.C.E. As to which of the two languages was the original, they permit no sure conclusion.[9] This book is transmitted further not only in Greek, but also in Old Latin, Syriac, Armenian, and the Vulgate. As with the book of Judith, Jerome also knew an Aramaic text in use among the Jews. The Aramaic text preserved in a fifteenth-century manuscript, however, differs from Jerome's text because it does not offer a reliable form of the text and already renders the first-person report in 1:3–3:6 in the third person. Therefore, the text of the Septuagint remains the oldest completely attested form of the text. It is transmitted, however, in three versions: (1) in the long text G II transmitted by Codex Sinaiticus; (2) in the short text G I conveyed by Codices Vaticanus, Alexandrinus, and Venetus; and (3) in an intermediate version G III attested by two minuscule manuscripts and limited to 6:9–12:22. Although the question cannot be unequivocally determined whether the long text represents a secondarily expanded form of the short text or, conversely, the short text an abridged version of the long text, the likelihood, according to the exhaustive investigation by Robert Hanhart, is that the short text represents a secondary smoothing of the long text.[10] This conclusion is confirmed by the Qumran fragments, which attest the long text.

Thesis 2: Origin, Dating, and Provenance of the Book. The solution of the literary-critical problem of the book of Tobit is complicated by the fact that the complete text is extant only in translation. Nevertheless, the distinction can be made in the book at least between the narrative and a revision that inserted the song of thanksgiving in chapter thirteen and Tobit's advice in chapter fourteen.[11] Whether the book originated in the eastern Diaspora, Egypt, or Palestine remains unclear. The hypothesis forwarded by Josef T. Milik and Merten Rabenau[12] that the core narrative stems from

---

[8] Compare the inventory in J. Maier, *Die Qumran-Essener: Die Texte vom Toten Meer II* (UTB 1863; Munich: Reinhardt, 1995), 137–38; J. A. Fitzmyer, "Fragments," *CBQ* 57 (1995), 655–75; and, succinctly, Moore, AB 40A, 34–39; or Ego, *JSHRZ*, 878–79. F. García Martínez, *The Dead Sea Scrolls Translated: The Qumran Texts in English* (Leiden: Brill, 1994), 293–99, offers an English translation of the fragments.

[9] See, most recently, Moore, AB 40A, 38–39 and 60, as well as Ego, *JSHRZ* 2.6, 880–81.

[10] See, too, Ego's (*JSHRZ*, 2.6, 875 n. 5) review of the conclusions reached in the history of research since the middle of the last century. It can be supplemented by the references in Moore, AB 40A, 58, who, like Rabenau, *Studien*, 3–7, has declared for the priority of G II.

[11] Compare also Moore, AB 40A, 22.

[12] See also H. Engel, "Tobit," 254.

Samarian circles deserves consideration. In its current shape, however, a Judaic-Jerusalemite perspective governs the book so that its final revision is to be located in Jerusalem or Judah. The recognition of the prophetic books as Holy Scriptures in 14:4 constitutes the *terminus post quem*. The motif of the slain Jews probably mirrors the experiences of religious persecution in the time of Antiochus IV. It may, however, as Merten Rabenau suggests, come from the hand of an editor. Therefore, it seems reasonable to date the core narrative to the third and the expansions to the second century B.C.E.

Issue 5: Literary Criticism of the Book. Since the analyses by Paul Deselaers and Merten Rabenau there can be no doubt that the book attained its present form only after a long literary development. Thus, for example, the Ahiqar episode in 1:18–21 (see also 2:10*), foreshadowed in 1:15, notably represents a delay in the plot development with the dual purpose of establishing a connection to the Ahiqar account, beloved in Jewish circles (as the book of Judith shows), and of strengthening the picture of a righteous person suffering for the sake of his piety. By introducing the kings Sennacherib and Esarhaddon, the editor demonstrates his dependence on the Aramaic book of Ahiqar. Even if one can assume that the book of Ahiqar served as a model for the insertion of speeches of admonition into the narrative, the episode mentioned seems to involve a more recent insertion. In addition, 1:4–8, 10–11 and 2:6–8 stand out from their context as pro-Jerusalemite as well as oriented toward the theology of the Law and the Prophets. Chapters 13 and 14 show, moreover, that there was an Ahiqar and a Jerusalem revision. First, the prayer in 13:1–14:1 already stands out from its surroundings as an insertion interested in the Diaspora and Zion theology and explicitly identifying the supplicant, who goes unnamed in the long text. In chapter 14, it is remarkable from the outset that the total age of Tobit is mentioned in v. 2a before his age when healed in v. 2b. With Tobit's brief farewell and the comments concerning the death and burial of him and his wife, after which Tobias moves to his father-in-law, Raguel, vv. 11–15 reveal themselves as the core of the continued narrative. Apparently, this move to Media is based secondarily in the unrighteousness of the region as illustrated by Ahiqar's fate. Finally, vv. 3b–7 offer an additional reason by citing Nahum's prediction of the fall of Assur and Nineveh (cf. 15a). Therefore, at least a core narrative, an Ahiqar recension, and a Jerusalem recension may be distinguished in the book. Moreover, the core narrative takes the motif of Shalmaneser V's exile of the Israelites to Assyria and Media from 2 Kgs 17:3, 6.

Comment 2: The Source-Critical Theories of Paul Deselaers and Merten Rabenau. Paul Deselaers attempts to solve the source problem by assuming a threefold process of growth.[13] He starts with G I as the presumed basic text of the book and attributes to it barely 50 percent of the book; he dates G I to the middle of the third century in Alexandria. The first revision occurred around 220 B.C.E. in Jerusalem in an effort to intensify the didactic content through recourse to the Law and the Prophets. A second revision was undertaken only two decades later, presumably in Alexandria once again and possibly under the influence of the atmosphere of pogrom reigning there. This revision introduced Ahiqar into the narrative. The third and last revision took place around 185 B.C.E., again in Jerusalem, and may have already represented an apocalypticizing eschatology. Deselaers thus intends to do justice both to the Greek short text and the original, wherein lies the problematic aspects of his analysis.

As a result, Merten Rabenau reexamined the long text. On the basis of careful observations of inner tensions and stylistic variations, he came to the conclusion that a base narrative and three successive revisions can be distinguished: the first revision had a clearly ethicizing tendency that underscored Tobit's piety, made use of corresponding generalizations, and transformed Tobit into a Galilean adherent of the Jerusalem temple. In addition, it inserted the song of thanksgiving in 13:1–8*. The second revision extensively expanded the text, introduced Ahiqar, and juxtaposed Hannah's faintheartedness against Tobit's suffering. The third revision, apart from the insertion of 1:3–8* and 13:6i–l, 9–18, merely glossed the text. Thus Rabenau dates the core narrative to the third century B.C.E., and contrary to the usual locating of the book in the Diaspora or Judea, he joins Josef T. Milik in considering an origin in Samaria possible.[14] The revisions were undertaken, then, in Jewish circles, and the second and third also certainly in Palestine between the middle and end of the second century.[15] Even if one takes seriously Beate Ego's reminder that source critical conclusions based on stylistic observations may only be drawn on the basis of the original text,[16] it is hardly accidental that the two most recent source-critical analyses reach comparable conclusions, namely, in distinguishing a total of four literary layers from one another.

---

[13] Deselaers, *Tobit,* 374–500; compare the summary, 501–15.

[14] See J. T. Milik, "La patrie de Tobie," *RB* 73 (1966): 522–30; and Rabenau, *Studien,* 177–82.

[15] Rabenau, *Studien,* 149–90.

[16] *JSHRZ* 2.6, 890.

Issue 6: Age and Provenance of the Book. The discussion concerning the age and provenance of the book has not yet led to an unequivocal result. The core narrative with its action played out in the eastern Diaspora supports the assumption that it also originated in the Diaspora. Therefore, Egypt, Syria, and Mesopotamia have been suggested as its home, although this assumption is not conclusive, since the narrator could have sought such a milieu for his adventure-rich and, at the same time, pious account. Since the demon flees to Egypt according to the long text of 8:6, which is to be regarded original, its origin in this country may be excluded. Only the short text has him carried, bound, to upper Egypt and thereby has taken into account the Alexandrian Diaspora. Noteworthy, however, is the hypothesis proposed by Josef T. Milik and accepted by Merten Rabenau that Tobit was originally an inhabitant of a "Tebez" located in Samaria. A Judean redaction transformed him into a Naphtalite and thus to a member of a region that later adhered to the Jerusalem temple. This would, indeed, be the simplest way to explain how the hero of the account does not belong to the Jewish *golah*.[17] Since the Aramaic book of Ahiqar was already in the possession of the Jewish military colony at Elephantine at the end of the fifth century B.C.E., there is no need to assume a Syrian origin for the redaction of the book to explain its awareness of the Ahiqar story. Since the Jerusalem redaction does not seem to know the conquest and forced conversion of Galilee to Judaism by Aristobulus I (104 B.C.E.),[18] this version of Tobit can be no later than the last third of the second century B.C.E. In contrast, the upper limit of dating may be determined only with difficulty, since the core account could have originated anytime between the late Persian era and the beginning the second century B.C.E.

Issue 7: The Theology of the Book. In its fashion, this little book expresses belief in the righteousness of God, whose ways humans often cannot comprehend but who nonetheless graciously guides the pious and, in the end, delivers them from all dangers. Meanwhile, the pious stands the test by adhering to the Torah (1:6; 3:4), by reading in the prophetic books (2:6; 14:4), and by journeying to Jerusalem for pilgrimage feasts in accordance with the Torah, not only offering there the prescribed offerings, but also freely giving to the widows, orphans, and proselytes (1:6–8). In everyday life, he or she should follow the Golden Rule (4:15 G I), give the worker just wages, and use surplus goods for works of mercy by feeding the hungry, clothing the naked, and burying the dead (1:17; 4:16; 12:8).

---

[17] See Milik, "Patrie," 522–30; and Rabenau, *Studien*, 149, 189.
[18] Compare Schürer/Vermes 1:217–18.

Throughout all this, the pious person should constantly praise God and pray for his just guidance (see 4:19 with 3:2 and 3:11), for mercy delivers from death and cleanses from every sin (12:9). The prayers of the saints, however, are brought before God by the seven holy angels with access to the glory of the Holy One who then sends one of them to accompany his pious ones and to deliver them from all danger. That which occurs visibly in the narrative can take place invisibly in the life of every pious individual. The related concept of the death angel who, on God's command, calls one from this life (see Job 33:22) resounds in Sarah's prayer for her death in 3:13. Tobit's song of praise clearly addresses Diaspora Jews in order to hold out the prospect of a return home so that they could thank God in Jerusalem should they repent of their sins (13:16 G II; 13:1–7[8] G I). A summons to Jerusalem to praise God as is God's due follows immediately; after a prospective vision of her coming eternal glory, the call to praise his holy name in all eternity concludes the prayer.

Bibliography

Introduction:
Oesterley. *Introduction,* 161–71.
Eißfeldt. *Introduction,* 583–85.
Rost. *EinlApo,* 44–47.
Schürer/Vermes 3.1:222–32.
H. Engel. "Das Buch Tobit," in Zenger, *Einleitung,* 246–56.

The Text:
R. Hanhart. *Text und Textgeschichte des Buches Tobit.* AAWG 3.139. Göttingen: Vandenhoeck & Ruprecht, 1984.
J. A. Fitzmyer. "The Aramaic and Hebrew Fragments of Tobit from Qumran Cave 4." *CBQ* 57 (1995): 655–75 (with bibliography).

Issues:
S. Liljeblad. *Die Tobiasgeschichte und andere Märchen vom toten Helfer.* Lund: Lindstedts, 1927.
J. T. Milik. "La patrie de Tobie." *RB* 73 (1966): 522–30.
J. Gamberoni. *Die Auslegung des Buches Tobias in der griechisch-lateinischen Kirche der Antike und der Christenheit des Westens bis 1600.* SANT 21. Munich: Kösel, 1969.
L. Ruppert. "Das Buch Tobias: Ein Modellfall nachgestaltender Erzählung." Pages 109–19 in *Wort, Lied, Gottesspruch: FS J. Ziegler.* Edited by J. Schreiner. FB 1. Würzburg: Echter Verlag, 1972.

————. "Zur Funktion der Achikar-Notizen im Buch Tobias." *BZ* NS 20 (1976): 232–37.

P. Deselaers. *Das Buch Tobit: Studien zu seiner Entstehung, Komposition und Theologie.* OBO 43. Göttingen: Vandenhoeck & Ruprecht, 1982.

M. Rabenau. *Studien zum Buch Tobit.* BZAW 220. New York: de Gruyter, 1994.

Commentaries:
M. Löhr, *APAT,* 1900; D. C. Simpson, *APOT,* 1913; M. Schumpp, EHAT, 1933; A. Miller, HSAT, 1940; F. Stummer, EB, 1950; H. Bückers, HBK, 1953; F. Zimmermann, JAL, 1958; H. Gross, NEchtB, 1987; P. Deselaers, GS, 1990; C. A. Moore, AB, 1996; B. Ego, *JSHRZ,* 1999.

The Book of Judith

Thesis: The Literary Character of the Book. According to Erich Zenger, we encounter in the book of Judith a "novelistic account in didactic form."[19] Against the backdrop of a fictive historical framework, it develops a dramatic plot with multiple story lines that render the verdict as to whether the human ruler of world, who claims exclusive divinity, or Yahweh is the sole God. Yahweh's true deity is revealed in that a woman, equally pious and brave, employing erotic means while preserving her modesty, kills the general of the world ruler's army come to conquer the land and its capital, Jerusalem, and thereby delivers her people. Biblical motifs and historical figures work in tandem in the account and thus form a story that is intended to strengthen the self-understanding of Jews of the second half of the second century B.C.E. as the people of the sole God, Yahweh.

Issue 1: The Structure of the Book. The book may be divided into three parts:

Chapters 1–3: The thesis: Nebuchadnezzar's claim, based on his power, to be the true God.

Chapters 4–7: The alternative: Is Nebuchadnezzar or Yahweh the true God?

Chapters 8–16: The antithesis: Yahweh alone is God.

---

[19] E. Zenger, "Judith/Judithbuch," *TRE* 17:406; see Zenger, *JSHRZ* 1.6, 436–39; and regarding the discussion, Moore, AB 40, 71–76.

Part 1 (1:1–3:10): After the king of Assyria, Nabuchodosor (that is, Nebuchadnezzar), had conquered King Arphaxad of Media and the peoples of Asia and North Africa, he sent his general Holophernes against the coastal lands to subjugate them. After Holophernes with his armies had conquered Cilicia in the northwest, Japhet/Epha and Midian in the south, and the plain of Damascus in the middle, fear and terror gripped all the cities from Sidon to Ashkelon. Consequently, they subjected themselves to him and, in accordance with his demand, destroyed all their sanctuaries and idols "so that all the nations of the earth should serve Nebuchadnezzar alone and all tongues and tribes call upon him alone as God" (3:8).[20] Thus 3:8 states the theme: who is the true and only God?

Part 2 (4:1–7:32): In narrative form, the second part again raises the question of whether this claim is appropriate for Nebuchadnezzar or for Yahweh. In view of the departure of the army from the Plain of Jezreel to conquer Samaria and Jerusalem, the high priest Jehoiakim called on the inhabitants of Bethulia and Betomesthaim, located at the northern limits of the Samarian mountains, to place their cities on the defensive and to bar the enemy's path into the mountains. Achior, the leader of the Ammonites, explained to Holophernes, astounded at the resistance, with which people and God he was involved. He warned him unsuccessfully against an attack. One can only vanquish this people if it has transgressed against its God; otherwise, the attacker becomes a mockery (5:20–21).

Part 3 (8:1–16:25): The third part gives the answer expected after Achior's words. When the beautiful, well-to-do, and pious widow, Judith, heard of Holophernes' decision to attack Israel nonetheless, she summoned the elders of Bethulia to reproach them for their lack of faith and, summarizing Israel's past and present, proudly confessed in 8:20: "We know no other God than him [that is, the Lord] only. Therefore, we hope that he will not abandon us and our race." Then she prayed to the Lord, in conclusion calling upon him to cause "your people and every nation to recognize and know that you alone are God, the God of all power and might, and that there is no other protector for your people Israel than you" (10:14).

Then she went, as she had announced, to the enemy camp. When she was brought at her request before Holophernes, she duplicitously promised that if he would follow her words, God would complete the work through him and nothing that he intended would remained unfulfilled (11:6). She justified her desertion by the lawlessness planned in the city for which they were already seeking emergency permission in Jerusalem. If

---

[20] Citations follow Zenger, *JSHRZ* 1.6.

they obtain it and act accordingly, the destruction of the city will be certain. Without sinning by partaking of unclean foods, she remained in the enemy camp until, on the fourth night, she allowed Holofernes' eunuch Bagoas to talk her into visiting the general in his tent. Even here, however, she preserved her purity, for the drunken Holofernes was incapable of an act of love. Thus, Judith's hour was come. She decapitated the sleeper and fled with his head to Bethulia.

With the cry, "Our God is with us, yes, our God is with us yet, showing power in Israel and strength against our enemies, as he has today!" she demanded entry into the city (13:11). Then the inhabitants of Bethulia summoned Achior, whom Holofernes had handed over to them after his supposed traitorous advice (6:10–21). When he saw Holofernes' head, he praised Judith, underwent circumcision, and thus entered the house of Israel (13:6–10). When the enemy army saw the head of its general hanging on the wall the next morning it fled in panic. The inhabitants of delivered Bethulia, however, followed Judith, leading them with a song of thanksgiving, in festive procession to Jerusalem. Having arrived there, she donated to the temple as the requisite thanksgiving sacrifice booty from the tent of the fallen. The thanksgiving festival of the whole nation lasted three months, after which each returned to his inheritance. Judith, however, continued to live as a chaste and pious widow in Bethulia. When, at the age of 105 years, her end approached, she freed her slave, died, and was buried in the burial cave of her husband. Indeed, as long as she lived and for many years after her death, no enemy dared to frighten Israel.

Issue 2: Historical Fiction, Historical and Biblical Reminiscences. Judith 1:1 already shows anyone who knows the history of Israel and of the ancient Near East that Judith is fiction, for the neo-Babylonian king Nebuchadnezzar II was neither king of Assyria, nor did he reside in Nineveh, nor did he conquer the Medes. To the contrary, he felt it necessary to erect a protective wall against them in order to keep them at a distance from his realm. On the other hand, we encounter the generals Orofernes and Bagoas, whom we meet in the story as Holofernes and his attendant Bagoas, in the entourage of the Persian king Artaxerxes III Ochos, who, indeed, subjugated Phoenicia and reconquered Sidon and Egypt a last time for the Persian Empire in 345/4 B.C.E. With equal speed, one knowledgeable of Israelite-Jewish history sees through the historical fiction that the Judeans deported in 597 or 586, respectively, had already returned in the seventeenth year of Nebuchadnezzar (588/7), that, in the meanwhile, the temple had been newly consecrated (4:3), and that a high priest stood at the head of the Jewish community. Neither can the city, Bethulia (*bêt ʾĔlôhā*, "house of God") be found on any map. One can, however, hear in Nebuchadnezzar's impudent claim and in the account of the destruction of the sanctuaries of conquered lands an echo of the profanation of the Jerusalem temple in the years of religious persecution by Antiochus IV (168–165 B.C.E.). In a similar fashion, the Seleucid general Nicanor, defeated by Judas Maccabeus, may lurk behind the figure of Holofernes.

Biblical motifs are so numerous that they can only be enumerated here in outline and only for Judith herself.[21] Obviously, Judith is portrayed as a second Jael and Deborah (Judg 5). When she decapitates Holofernes, the account of David and Goliath (1 Sam 17) also shimmers through. Furthermore, Judith bears features of Miriam, who sounds a song of thanksgiving after the deliverance at the sea (Exod 15:20–21). Finally, Achior is clearly none other than the wise Ahiqar whom we know from the Aramaic papyrus found in Elephantine.[22]

Issue 3: The Theology and Piety of the Book. The book of Judith is a confession of Yahweh's unique divinity in narrative form. His divinity is manifest in Israel, even in the face of overpowering enemies, in the success of human acts of liberation prepared through prayer and fasting and executed in observance of all the ritual regulations of the Torah, unless there is an express dispensation from the high priest in Jerusalem. Thus, the booklet records positively the lessons learned by the followers of the Maccabees at the very beginning of the Jewish rebellion (see 1 Macc 2:31–41). Simultaneously, it represents the ideal of one people of Yahweh to which even the inhabitants of the Samarian mountains belong.

Issue 4: Age and Provenance. From what has been said to this point, it can be concluded that the period of religious persecution, the rededication of the temple, and Judas Maccabee's victory over Nicanor lie in the narrator's past. Consequently, the book must postdate 160. The reference in 2:28 to the coastal cities, considered no more a part of Jewish territory than was Galilee, establishes the *terminus ad quem.* Consequently, the book is older than Alexander Jannaeus's conquest of Galilee and the coastal region (103–76 B.C.E.). The fact that in the narrative the inhabitants of Samaria are subject to the Jerusalem high priest can be considered, following

---

[21] Compare Zenger, *JSHRZ* 1.6, 439–46.

[22] According to I. Kottsieper, *Die Sprache der Ahiqarsprüche* (BZAW 194; New York: de Gruyter, 1990), esp. 179; and I. Kottsieper, "Die Geschichte und die Sprüche des weisen Achiqar," in *Texte aus der Umwelt des Alten Testaments* (ed. O. Kaiser et al.; Gütersloh: Mohn, 1991), 3.2:320–47. Judging from the old Aramaic language, the sayings of Ahikar stem from the time between 750 and 650 B.C.E., while the framework narrative already belongs to Imperial Aramaic.

Carey A. Moore, an argument for a date after the destruction of the Samaritan temple in 128 B.C.E. and the ensuing annexation of Samaria by John Hyrcanus in 107 B.C.E.[23] In any case, one must seek the Torah-observant author in circles that opposed at a distance the Hasmoneans because of their dual role as high priests and princes commanding their army. Judith 4:6–8 has the high priest together with the council of the elders merely address a letter to the two cities responsible for barring entry to the Samarian mountains, but not appear himself in the theater of war. Rather, like all priests, he performs sacrificial duties wearing sackcloth (4:14). According to Zenger, the author may stem from Hasidic circles.[24] It is entirely possible that Moore is correct that the author belonged to the Pharisees[25] since, according to Josephus (*Ant.* 13.288–300), the conflict between them and the Hasmoneans was already building in the days of John Hyrcanus.

The novel represents as a matter of fact the ideal of an undivided Israel, led by the high priest and the council of elders, and dependent in times of war on the local militia and, especially, on God's help. Perhaps the destruction of the Samaritan temple or the conquest of Samaria encouraged the author to take this view. Yet an earlier date, not linked to Pharisaic authorship, cannot be excluded either. It is, therefore, difficult to determine the author's location. There are no compelling reasons to locate him outside Palestine. Whether one can conclude from Judith's benevolent attitude toward the Samaritans that the author was Samaritan must remain an open question in view of the programmatic character of the tale.[26] In contrast, Essene authorship can be excluded since not a single fragment of Judith survives among the fragments of several hundred scrolls discovered in the Qumran caves.

Issue 5: Language and the Transmission of the Text. The book of Judith has been transmitted in Greek, Latin, Syriac, and Armenian. Syntax and diction imply a Semitic, presumably Hebrew, original.[27] According to information in his *Prologus* to the book of Judith, at the end of the fourth century Jerome could still access for his translation a Chaldean version that Jews used at the time. The arguments of André Marie Dubarle notwithstanding, no revision of the Aramaic text available to Jerome underlies the

---

[23] Moore, AB 40, 67–68.

[24] So Zenger, "Judith/Judithbuch," 406.

[25] So Moore, AB 40, 70, who also refers to the attempt by H. Mantel ("Ancient Hasidim," *Studies in Judaism* [1976], 60–80 [Hebrew]) to locate the book in Sadducean circles, although the institutional and ritual reasons cited are insufficient.

[26] Compare, however, Moore, AB 40, 71, who leaves the question undecided.

[27] See the lists in Zenger, *JSHRZ* 1.6, 430–31; and Moore, AB 40, 66–67.

various Hebrew recensions of the book in circulation in the Middle Ages. It is more likely a retroversion related to the text of the Vulgate and to Greek secondary traditions. According to Robert Hanhart, among the divergent Greek recensions, those of Codices Vaticanus, Alexandrinus, Venetus, and the fragmentary Sinaiticus, preserved only in 11:13–13:8, attest to the most reliable form of the text.

Bibliography

Introduction:
Oesterley. *Introduction,* 172–82.
Eißfeldt. *Introduction,* 585–87.
Rost. *EinlApo,* 38–41.
Schürer/Vermes 3.1:216–22.
E. Zenger. "Judith/Judithbuch," *TRE* 17:404–8.
H. Engel. "Das Judithbuch," in Zenger, *Einleitung,* 256–66.

The Text:
A. M. Dubarle. *Judith: Formes et sens des diverses traditions.* AnBib 24/1–2. Rome: Pontifical Biblical Institute, 1966.
———. "Les textes hébreux de Judith et les étapes de la formation du livre." *Bib* 70 (1989): 255–66.
R. Hanhart. *Text und Textgeschichte des Buches Judith.* AAWG 3/109. Göttingen: Vandenhoeck & Ruprecht, 1979.
H. Engel. "Der HERR ist ein Gott, der Kriege zerschlägt: Zur Frage der griechischen Originalsprache und der Struktur des Buches Judit." Pages 155–68 in *Goldene Äpfel in silbernen Schalen: Collected Communications to the XIIIth Congress of the International Organization for the Study of the Old Testament.* Edited by K.-D. Schunck and M. Augustin. BEATAJ 20. New York: Lang, 1992.

Issues:
E. Haag. *Studien zum Buche Judith: Seine theologische Bedeutung und literarische Eigenart.* TThSt 16. Trier: Paulinus, 1963.
E. Zenger. "Der Juditroman als Traditionsmodell des Jahweglaubens." *TTZ* 83 (1974): 65–80.
H. Y. Pribatsch. "Das Buch Judith und seine hellenistischen Quellen." *ZDPV* 90 (1974): 50–60.
L. Alonso Schökel and W. Wuellner, eds. *Narrative Structures in the Book of Judith.* Colloquy 11. Berkeley: Center for Hermeneutical Studies in Hellenistic and Modern Culture, 1975.

T. Craven. *Artistry and Faith in the Book of Judith.* SBLDS 70. Chico: Scholars Press, 1983.

I. Kottsieper, *Die Sprache der Ahiqarsprüche.* BZAW 194. New York: de Gruyter, 1990.

———. "Die Geschichte und die Sprüche des weisen Achiqar." Pages 320–47 in *Texte aus der Umwelt des Alten Testaments.* Vol. 3.2. Edited by O. Kaiser et al. Gütersloh: Mohr, 1991.

J. C. VanderKam, ed. *"No One Spoke Ill of Her": Essays on Judith.* Early Judaism and Its Literature 2. Atlanta: Scholars Press, 1992.

J. W. van Henten. "Judith as an Alternative Leader: A Reading of Judith 7–13." Pages 224–52 in *A Feminist Companion to Esther, Judith and Susanna.* Edited by A. Brenner. Sheffield: Sheffield Academic Press, 1995.

Commentaries:
M. Löhr, *APAT,* 1900; A. E. Cowley, *APOT,* 1913; A. Miller, HSAT, 1940; F. Stummer, EB, 1950 (1954³); M. Enslin, JAL, 1972; J. Dancy, CBC, 1972; E. Zenger, *JSHRZ,* 1980; C. A. Moore, AB, 1985; H. Gross, NEchtB, 1987; E. Haag, GS, 1995.

The Additions to the Greek Book of Esther

Thesis: The book of Esther gives only indirect indication in its report that God delivered the Jews from an empire-wide pogrom in the time of King Ahasuerus/Xerxes, which his Jewish spouse Esther was able to avert thanks to the advice of her uncle Mordecai. This was soon perceived as a lack that the six additions transmitted in the Septuagint, designated A-F in the literature, sought to remedy.[28] On closer examination, it becomes apparent that the additions trace back to two different circles of tradition, of which, the older, Egyptian tradition underscored the loyalty between the foreign king and the Jews while the younger, Palestinian tradition aimed at a transparent theologization.

Issue 1: The Expansions A 1–11, C, and F 1–11. The two related expansions, A at the beginning and F at the end of the book, contain the report of Mordecai's dream (A 1–11), his discovery of a conspiracy against Xerxes (A 12–176), and the dream's interpretation, perceived only after its fulfillment, along with a colophon (F 1–11). The insertion after Esth 3:17,

---

[28] Regarding the additions in the Old Latin, see I. Kottsieper, ATD 5, 133.

which, according to Carey A. Moore and Ingo Kottsieper, stems from the same revision, offers the prayers of Mordecai and Esther asking the Lord both to spare his people from the massacre that Haman planned (C 1–11) and to give Esther strength before her appearance before the king so that the idol's reputation could be annihilated (C 12–30). Both prayers rely on communal laments from the time of the religious persecution of Antiochus IV. Of the expansions, A 1–11, C 1–30, and F 1–10 (11) seem, according to Kottsieper, to trace back to a Semitic text available to the Greek translators. The Greek translation presumably originated during the final years of the reign of King Alexander Jannaeus (103–76 B.C.E.) in Pharisaic circles in Palestine.

Issue 2: The Additions A 12–17, B, D 1–12, and E. These additions may be connected. A 12–17 represents a parallel version of Esth 2:21–23. The related D 1–12 reports the appearance of the queen before Xerxes and serves as a substitute for 5:1–2. The two royal documents, B (which confirms the pogrom) and E, come from the same revision.[29] All these texts emphasize loyalty to the foreign king.[30] Consequently, they presuppose a Diaspora situation which, according to Moore[31] and Kottsieper,[32] the colophon (F 11) locates during the reign of Ptolemy VIII Euergetes II (126–116 B.C.E.) in Egypt, where there was a form of the text of Esther independent of the Palestinian.

Issue 3: The Text of the Septuagint and of the Vulgate. Additions 1 and 2 show that the Septuagint text represents the incorporation of the peculiarities of the Palestinian text into the Egyptian version. The transition between the base text and the addition is smoothed only in the case of C and D through the insertion of D 13–15, which corresponds to C's characterization of Esther. Whoever prays for the manifestation of the exclusive divinity of the Lord may not bow to any human being. Since the Palestinian revision (before 76 B.C.E.) established the *terminus a quo* and the acquaintance of 3 Maccabees with the Septuagint form of the book of Esther the *terminus ad quem* (70 C.E.), a date in the second half of the first century, the arithmetic average, seems likely.[33] The text of the Vulgate conforms to that of the Septuagint, but places the additions, labeled as such, at the end of the book.

---

[29] See also C. A. Moore, AB 44, 166.
[30] See Kottsieper, ATD 5, 120–21.
[31] Moore, AB 44, 166.
[32] Kottsieper, ATD 5, 123.
[33] But see Kottsieper, ATD 5, 125, who suggests 50 B.C.E.

Comment 1: The Transmission of the Text. The Greek text of the book is best transmitted in the long form of Codices Vaticanus, Sinaiticus, and Alexandrinus. In addition, another Greek version exists in the (Lucianic) short form A, which included the additions only secondarily. Its variations in the additions are further developments of the Septuagint text.[34]

Bibliography

Introduction:
Oesterley. *Introduction,* 183–95.
Eißfeldt. *Introduction,* 591–92.
Rost. *EinlApo,* 61–64.
J. van der Klaauw. "Das Griechische Estherbuch." *TRE* 10:394.
Schürer/Vermes 3.2:718–22.

The Text:
H. J. Cook. "The A Text of the Greek Versions of the Book of Esther," *ZAW* 81 (1969): 369–71.
R. A. Martin. "Syntax Criticism of the LXX Additions to the Book of Esther," *JBL* 94 (1975): 65–72.
E. Tov. "The 'Lucianic' Text of the Canonical and the Apocryphal Sections of Esther: A Rewritten Biblical Book." *Textus* 10 (1982): 1–25.

The Issues:
E. L. Ehrlich. "Der Traum des Mordechai." *ZRGG* 7 (1955): 69–74.
C. A. Moore. "On the Origins of the LXX Additions to the Book of Esther," *JBL* 92 (1973): 382–93.
D. J. A. Clines. *The Esther Scroll: The Story of a Story.* JSOTSup 30. Sheffield: JSOT Press, 1984.
L. M. Wills, *The Jew in the Court of the Foreign King: Ancient Jewish Court Legends.* HDR 26. Minneapolis: Fortress, 1990.
M. V. Fox. *The Redaction of the Book of Esther: On Reading Composite Texts.* SBLMS 40. Atlanta: Scholars Press, 1991.

Commentaries:
V. Ryssel, *APAT,* 1900; J. A. F. Gregg, *APOT,* 1913; L. Paton, ICC, 1908; J. Schildenberger, HSAT, 1940; F. Stummer, EB, 1950; W. Fuerst, CBC, 1972;

---

[34] See H. J. Cook, "The A Text of the Greek Versions of the Book of Esther," *ZAW* 81 (1969): 369–71; I. Kottsieper, ATD 5, 125–28, and for a brief history of the text of the book, E. Zenger, "Das Buch Ester," in Zenger, *Einleitung,* 267–68.

H. Bardtke, *JSHRZ*, 1973; A. Moore, AB, 1977; W. Dommershausen, NEchtB, 1980; I. Kottsieper, ATD, 1998.

The Additions to the Greek Book of Daniel

Thesis 1: The Additions in the Greek Daniel. The Greek text of Daniel is transmitted in two versions, a longer version in the Septuagint and a shorter one based on a revision in the form of the Theodotion text. The Greek text in both versions contains a series of insertions and additions in comparison to the Hebrew Bible. As to the first, it offers between 3:23 and 24 (M) a long insertion in the form of the Prayer of Azariah and the Song of the Three Young Men; as to the second, the accounts of Susanna and of Bel and the Dragon are sometimes placed separately after the book, sometimes prefixed to it, and sometimes appended. All texts may have originally been composed in Hebrew or Aramaic. While both accounts are dated in the literature, as a rule, to the second century B.C.E., Ingo Kottseiper has argued for placing the account of Bel and the Dragon in the first half of the fourth century on the assumption that it was composed from three originally independent units. The prayers emphasize the paradigmatic piety of Job's three friends; the Susanna story, Daniel's wisdom and righteousness, and the story of Daniel and the destruction of the Bel idol, his zeal for aniconic devotion to Yahweh alone.

Thesis 2: The Prayer of Azariah and the Song of the Three Young Men. In the Septuagint, the Prayer of Azariah in vv. 26–45 follows a brief insertion in vv. 24–25, and the Song of the Three Young Men in 3:52–90 appears after the interlude in vv. 46–51 that reports the angel's wondrous deliverance of the three men from the fiery furnace. After the transition in v. 91a, the narrative resumes where v. 24 (M) left off. Thus is becomes clear that the entire section 3:24–91a (G) represents a secondary expansion. As Ingo Kottsieper has shown, it arises from a text tradition independent of the Septuagint text.[35] For its part, this tradition has incorporated a communal lament from the time of religious persecution by Antiochus IV (vv. 26–45), a benediction stemming from the postexilic temple cult (vv. 52–56; cf. Ps 144), and a hymn, presumably stemming from the Hellenistic period (vv. 57–85, 90),[36] that calls all nature to praise the Lord.

---

[35] See Kottsieper, ATD 5, 221–24.

[36] See J. J. Collins, *Daniel* (Hermeneia; Philadelphia: Fortress, 1993), 202–3; and, regarding its character and origin in the cult of the Jerusalem temple, Kottsieper, ATD 5, 246–47.

Thereby, the three friends are shown to be paradigmatically pious Jews who, in danger, pray to God for deliverance and praise him afterward.

Issue 1: The Textual History of the Insertions in Chapter 3. Since, in contrast to what precedes and follows, v. 24 G calls the three friends by their Jewish names, Hananiah (Ananias), Azariah, and Mishael, instead of by their Babylonian names, Shadrach, Meshach, and Abednego, and in v. 48 the Babylonians are killed a second time by a flame lashing forth from the furnace (see v. 23 G = 22 M), it is clear that the expansion arises from an independent Greek tradition of Daniel 3.[37] In it, the three had already prayed after v. 24, even before they were cast into the oven. When they were cast into it, an angel drove the flame out of the oven so that they were delivered, but the Chaldeans standing nearby were consumed (vv. 47–51).

Issue 2: The Prayer of Azariah. The Prayer of Azariah in Dan 3:26–45 G consists of a communal lament introduced by a judgment doxology, a lament that has no inherent relationship to the context (compare vv. 29–30). From the complaint, raised in v. 31, that the supplicants find themselves handed over to their apostate Jewish enemies and a godless king (v. 31) and from the entreaty, pronounced in v. 40, that God would accept their prayers in the place of burnt offerings and sacrifices, it is evident that the song stems from the period of religious persecution by Antiochus IV that lasted from 168 to 165.[38] He also prohibited the traditional sacrifices to Yahweh in the Jerusalem temple. A mistranslation in v. 40 permits the inference that the prayer was translated from Hebrew into Greek.[39]

Issue 3: The Song of the Three Young Men in the Fiery Furnace. The Song of the Three Young Men in 3:53–90 consists of a benediction of Yahweh (vv. 53–56) and a hymn (vv. 57–85, 90)[40] incorporated into its context by vv. 86–89. The benediction distinguishes between the temple as the seat of Yahweh's glory (*doxa/kabôd,* v. 53a) and heaven as his throne (v. 55a), while the Priestly document portrays the glory of Yahweh as the form of Yahweh's earthly manifestation.[41] Therefore, the Song could not have originated before the late Persian period. The appended hymn calls the entire creation, from the angels in heaven to his earthly servants, to praise God.

---

[37] See Kottsieper, ATD 5, 221–22 and 226.
[38] See Collins, *Daniel,* 202–3; and Kottsieper, ATD 5, 222 and 233–34.
[39] Kottsieper, ATD 5, 222 and 234 n.102.
[40] In distinction to Collins (*Daniel,* 202–3), who disputes the independence of the benediction. Contrariwise, Kottsieper (ATD 5, 241–42) judges it an originally independent liturgical text.
[41] See Kaiser, *GAT* II, 191–96.

Since the spirits and souls of the righteous are called to praise God only in v. 86, at the beginning of the insertion serving to adapt the hymn to its context, the hymn may stem from the late Persian or early Hellenistic period, and the insertion itself may date to the Maccabean period.

Thesis 3: The accounts of Susanna and Bel and the Dragon. The accounts of Susanna and of Bel and the Dragon are preserved in two versions, the older in the Septuagint and the younger in the Theodotion text, which abbreviates the accounts. The first account places Susanna in the foreground while the Septuagint version accentuates the distinction between the young and the old.[42] The Theodotion text underlies modern translations of the Bible. In the Septuagint both accounts follow Dan 12:13; in the Theodotion text, in contrast, the account of Susanna is prefixed to the book because Daniel still appears in it as a young man.[43] In terms of content, the Susanna narrative, in both its recensions, mirrors Palestinian Judaism's dispute in the second and first centuries over the question of the criteria applicable in judicial cases. As is still evident in the Septuagint version, Bel and the Dragon consists of three individual accounts: (1) the Dragon and Daniel in the lion's den, (2) Daniel's conviction of the priests of Bel, and (3) the prophet Habakkuk's visit to Daniel in Babylon. All the tales mentioned here may have originally been composed in Hebrew or Aramaic.

Issue 4: The Susanna Narrative. The story of Susanna, comprising sixty-four verses, relates the deliverance of the young wife of a Jew named Jehoiakim living in Babylon at the time of King Nebuchadnezzar through the wisdom of the young Daniel. After she had been condemned to death on the false witness of two Jewish elders she had spurned after they had spied on her bathing, Daniel succeeded in convicting the two witnesses as perjurers by interviewing them separately. As a result, they were executed instead of Susanna. The account is extant in two different recensions in the Septuagint and Theodotion. The beginning of the Septuagint version has been lost.[44] According to Ingo Kottsieper, the Septuagint version conceals an already complex account, originally written in Hebrew or

---

[42] Collins, *Daniel,* 427.

[43] See also G. Vermes and M. Goodman, "The Additions to Daniel," in Schürer/ Vermes 3.2:722–30, who both discuss the problem of the original language of the accounts and catalogue the use of the additions in patristic literature.

[44] See H. Engel, *Die Susannaerzählung: Einleitung, Übersetzung und Kommentar zum Septuagint-Text und zur Theodotion-Bearbeiten* (OBO 61; Göttingen: Vandenhoeck & Ruprecht, 1985), 55–77 and 78–136; and Kottsieper, ATD 5, 287–300.

Aramaic. Its beginning lost, it attained final form in the second century
B.C.E. in devout Palestinian circles. The Theodotion version replaces the
opposition between the elders and the righteous youths,[45] central to the
Septuagint account, with that between the true elders and the youths.
Thus, according to Ingo Kottsieper, it may mirror the conflict between the
Sadducees and the Pharisees in the time of the reign of the Hasmonean
queen Salome Alexandra (76–67 B.C.E.) and, therefore, stem from Saddu-
cean circles.[46]

Issue 5: The Account of Bel and the Dragon. The dual account of Bel and the
Dragon reports first in vv. 1–22 how the pious Daniel, who revered only
the one God and lived at the court of the king (Theodotion: of Cyrus), ex-
posed in the presence of the king the deceitful machinations of the priests
of Bel with the sacrifices intended for their god. Thereupon, the king killed
them while Daniel destroyed the statue and the temple of Bel. In vv. 23–42,
there follows the account of Daniel's slaying of a dragon worshiped by the
Babylonians and of Daniel's seven-day exposure in a lion pit by the king
responding to popular pressure. The prophet Ambakum (Habakkuk), on
God's command, fed Daniel in the pit. The king released him on the
seventh day. Thereupon, his enemies were thrown to the lions and
immediately consumed.

The Septuagint version, with its flawed transitions, shows that the account consists of the three originally independent stories of Daniel's conviction of the deceitful machinations of the priest of Bel, of Daniel's
slaying of the dragon and his subsequent deliverance from the lion's den,[47]
and of the prophet Habakkuk's provision for Daniel. Whereas up until
now it has usually been dated to the second century, Ingo Kottsieper places
it in the first half of the fourth century. Because the dragon represents the
god Marduk, the account of Daniel in the lion's den may have already
originated in the Babylonian *golah* before Xerxes' destruction of the Babylonian temple of Marduk in the year 482. Since the account presumes a
cordial relationship between the Jews and the foreign overlords, it belongs,
as John J. Collins argues, in the period before the religious edict of
Antiochus IV.[48] According to Kottsieper, the account of Habakkuk feeding

---

[45] Kottsieper, ATD 5, 282–83; see also E. Haag, *Daniel* (NEchtB; Wurzburg: Echter,
1993), 90 nn. 62–64; and Engel, *Susannaerzählung,* 179–80.

[46] See Engel, *Susannaerzählung,* 181–82, and Kottsieper, ATD 5, 292–94.

[47] Concerning its priority in relation to Dan 6, see K. Koch, *Deuterokanonische
Zusätze zum Danielbuch: Entstehung und Textgeschichte I–II* (AOAT 38/1–2; Neukirchen:
Neukirchen-Vluyn, 1987), 194–200; Collins, *Daniel,* 264; and Kottsieper, ATD 5, 256–58.

[48] Collins, *Daniel,* 418.

Daniel also dates as early as the fifth century. It would have originated in Palestine and would have promoted reconciliation between Palestinian Jewry and the *golah*.[49]

Bel is an old nickname for the Babylonian patron deity Marduk. As a result, the Bel narrative could, in Ingo Kottsieper's judgment, reflect the destruction of the temple of Marduk by Xerxes I in 482 B.C.E. In its older Septuagint version, it was concerned with proving that Bel is not a living god; in the younger version of the Theodotion text, with the invalidity of the idol images. The restraint of the account with respect to the bloody sacrifice, manifest in the remarkably limited realization of the quantities foreseen in Ezek 46 in relation to vegetable sacrifices, speaks for an origin in the Persian period. That the narrator does not have firsthand knowledge of the Babylonian cult is evident in the fact that the sacrificial materials correspond to the instructions in Ezek 46. Therefore, an origin in Palestine, as Ingo Kottsieper suggests, cannot be excluded.[50] Since the assessment of the age and origin of the account depends on the difficult problems of its relationship to Dan 6, the age of the book of Habakkuk, and the religio-historical classification of the derision of the pagan practice of feeding the gods, no uniform opinion regarding the age and origin of the whole narrative and its parts will quickly emerge in research.[51]

Bibliography

Introduction:
Oesterley. *Introduction*, 272–93.
Eißfeldt. *Introduction*, 588–90.
Rost. *EinlApo*, 64–69.
Schürer/Vermes 3.2:722–30.
H. Niehr. "Das Buch Daniel," in Zenger, *Einleitung*, 464–66.

The Text:
J. Schüpphaus. "Das Verhältnis des LXX- und Theodotion-Text in den apokryphen Zusätzen zum Danielbuch." *ZAW* 83 (1971): 49–72.

---

[49] Kottsieper, ATD 5, 255.
[50] Kottsieper, ATD 5, 253–54.
[51] To illustrate the breadth of the opinions currently held, one may call attention to the fact that A. Wysny, *Die Erzählungen von Bel und dem Drachen: Untersuchung zu Dan 14* (SBB 33; Stuttgart: Katholisches Bibelwerk, 1996), judges the whole story to be a didactic narrative that originated in Alexandria between 145 and 88 B.C.E., was composed in Greek, and countered Jewish tendencies to assimilate.

A. Geissen. *Der Septuaginta-Text des Buches Daniel Kap. 5–12 zusammen mit Susanna, Bel et Draco sowie Esther Kap.1,1–2,15 nach dem Kölner Teil des Papyrus 967.* PTA 5. Bonn: Habelt, 1968.

W. Hamm. *Der Septuagintatext des Buches Daniel Kap. 3–4 nach dem Kölner Teil des Papyrus 967.* PTA 21. Bonn: Habelt, 1977.

K. Koch. *Deuterokanonische Zusätze zum Danielbuch: Entstehung und Textgeschichte I–II.* AOAT 38.1–2. Neukirchen-Vluyn: Neukirchener, 1987.

Issues:

C. Kuhl. *Die drei Männer im Feuer (Daniel Kapitel 3 und seine Zusätze): Ein Beitrag zur israelitsche-jüdischen Literaturgeschichte.* BZAW 55. Giessen: Töpelmann, 1930.

F. Zimmermann. "Bel and the Dragon." *VT* 8 (1958): 438–40.

———. "The Story of Susanna and Its Original Language." *JQR* 48 (1957/1958): 236–41.

W. Baumgartner. "Susanna: Die Geschichte einer Legende." Pages 43–66 in *Zum Alten Testament und seiner Umwelt: Ausgewählte Aufsätze.* Edited by W. Baumgartner. Leiden: Brill, 1959.

M. Gilbert. "La prière d'Azarias." *NRTh* 96 (1974): 561–82.

H. Engel, *Die Susannaerzählung: Einleitung, Übersetzung und Kommentar zum Septuagint-Text und zur Theodotion-Bearbeitung.* OBO 61. Göttingen: Vandenhoeck & Ruprecht, 1985.

H. D. Preuß. *Verspottung fremder Religionen im Alten Testament.* BWANT 92. Stuttgart: Kohlhammer, 1971.

M. Heltzer. "The Story of Susanna and the Self-Government of the Jewish Community in Babylonia." *AION* 41 (1981): 35–39.

L. M. Wills, *The Jew in the Court of the Foreign King: Ancient Jewish Court Legends.* HDR 26. Minneapolis: Fortress, 1990.

M. J. Steussy. *Gardens in Babylon: Narrative and Faith in the Greek Legends of Daniel.* SBLDS 141. Atlanta: Scholars Press, 1993.

A. Wysny. *Die Erzählungen von Bel und dem Drachen: Untersuchung zu Dan 14.* SBB 33. Stuttgart: Katholisches Bibelwerk, 1996.

T. J. Meadowcroft. *Aramaic Daniel und Greek Daniel: A Literary Comparison.* JSOTSup 198. Sheffield: Sheffield Academic Press, 1997.

Commentaries:

J. Rothstein, *APAT,* 1900; T. W. Davies, *APOT,* 1913; O. Plöger, *JSHRZ,* 1973; A. Moore, AB, 1977; J. Collins, Herm, 1993; E. Haag, NEchtB, 1993; D. Bauer, NSKAT, 1996; I. Kottsieper, ATD, 1998.

4

Deuterocanonical Prophetic Books

The Book of Baruch

Thesis 1: The Book of Baruch as a Pseudepigraph. The Septuagint transmits the book of Baruch after Jeremiah and before Lamentations (Threni). It is also called 1 Baruch in contrast to the Syriac *Apocalypse of Baruch (2 Baruch)*[1] and the Greek *Apocalypse of Baruch (3 Baruch)*.[2] It could have originally been an expansion of the Greek book of Jeremiah or of its Hebrew exemplar before it was separated as an independent booklet in the course of further development. According to its superscription in 1:1–2, the scribe Baruch ben Neriah, known from the book of Jeremiah as the prophet's assistant, should be regarded as the author of the booklet. He is supposed to have committed it to writing in the fifth year of King Jehoiachin or the first of the deportation (597 B.C.E.) in Babylon and there read it before the king and the people. Thereupon, the hearers are supposed to have immediately done penitence, fasted, prayed, and sent the booklet, together with a monetary contribution and a cover letter recommending the public reading of the book, to the high priest Jehoiachim in Jerusalem. Although the *sopher* or scribe Baruch ben Neriah is a historical figure as evidenced by a seal impression found in Tell Bet Mirsim,[3] its attestation and character permit no doubt as to the pseudepigraphical character of the book.

Issue 1: The Unhistorical Character and the Literary Intention of the Book.[4] The superscription and the introduction of the book already contradict

---

[1] See A. F. J. Klijn, *Die syrische Baruch-Apokalypse* (*JSHRZ* 5.2; Gütersloh: Mohn, 1976), 103–84; or A. F. J. Klijn, "2 (Syriac Apocalypse of) Baruch (Early Second Century A.D.)," *OTP* 1:615–52.

[2] See W. Hage, *Die griechische Baruch-Apokalypse* (*JSHRZ* 5.1; Gütersloh: Mohn, 1979), 15–44; or H. E. Gaylord, "3 (Greek Apocalypse of) Baruch (First to Third Century A.D.)," *OTP* 1:653–79.

[3] G. I. Davies et al., *Ancient Hebrew Inscriptions: Corpus and Concordance* (New York: Cambridge University Press, 1991), no. 105.509, 186; translation and discussion, *Texte aus der Umwelt des Alten Testaments* 2.4 (ed. O. Kaiser et al.; Gütersloh: Mohn, 1988), 565–66.

[4] See also C. A. Moore, AB 44, 256.

one another. According to 1:2, Baruch wrote the book during the conquest and burning of Jerusalem.[5] Nevertheless, the subsequent introduction assumes that an otherwise unattested high priest, Jehoiakim,[6] son of Hilkiah and grandson of Shallum, and thus a son of the high priest officiating at the time of the Josianic Reform (see 2 Kgs 23:5), was able to officiate in an undestroyed temple and to assemble the people. In contrast, 2:25 assumes the destruction of the temple. In addition, in contradiction to historical reality, 1:11–12 treats Belshazzar, as does Dan 5, as Nebuchadnezzar's son. Furthermore, according to the portrayal of the book of Jeremiah,[7] from which the narrator took the figure of Baruch, he was not deported to Babylon but like the prophet was abducted to Egypt.[8] As Pierre-Maurice Bogaert (1986) has already recognized, the introduction consciously depicts a picture that contrasts with the behavior of King Jehoiakim and the people in Jeremiah 36.[9] Consequently, it cannot be ruled out that the introduction first comprised an appendix to the book of Jeremiah and was only separated from it in order to be joined to 1:18–5:9.

Thesis 2: The Structure of the Book. The booklet, comprising five chapters, divides into three clearly distinct parts: A (1:1–3:8), B (3:9–4:4), and C (4:5–5:9). A is prose; B and C are poetry. The inner relationship of the three parts consists in the fact that the central idea in A, that only proper penitence can lead to Israel's redemption because the destruction of Jerusalem was the consequence of its failure to repent and its disobedience, is taken up in B in the summons to repent in obedience to the Torah as a condition for Israel's redemption. At the center of C stands a small lament and comfort liturgy in which the lament of Zion, personified as a woman, over the deportation of her children (4:9–10) and her song of comfort addressed to them (4:11–29) precede a word of comfort that promises

---

[5] The date of the fifth year and seventh month gives the impression of being a variant of the information in 2 Kgs 25:8—while simultaneously contrasting with Jer 36:9—which states that the temple was burned on the seventh day of the fifth month. For an extensive treatment of the problem, see O. H. Steck, *Das apokryphe Baruchbuch: Studien zu Rezeption und Konzentration "kanonischer" Überlieferung* (FRLANT 160; Göttingen: Vandenhoeck & Ruprecht, 1993), 17–20.

[6] Compare the lists of high priests in 1 Chr 5:29–41 with those in Ezra 3:2; 10:6; Neh 3:1, 20 and 12:10–11.

[7] See Jer 32:12–13, 16; 36:4–32; 43:3, 6; and 45:1–2.

[8] On the tendentious character of Jer 43:1–7, see K.-F. Pohlmann, *Studien zum Jeremiabuch* (FRLANT 118; Göttingen: Vandenhoeck & Ruprecht, 1978), 145–59 and 205; on the fictive authorship of the book of Baruch, see Steck, *Baruchbuch*, 303–5.

[9] See P.-M. Bogaert, "Le personnage de Baruch et l'histoire du livre de Jérémie: Aux origines du livre deutérocanonique de Baruch," in *Papers Presented to the Fifth International Congress on Biblical Studies Held at Oxford, 1973* (ed. E. A. Livingstone; Studia Evangelica 7/TU 126; Berlin: Akademie Verlag, 1982), 73–81.

Jerusalem that her prayer will soon be granted in the form of the annihilation of her enemies and the return of her children (4:30–5:9). Thus in its present form the book reveals itself to be a well-planned composition.

Thesis 3: The Literary Problem of the Book. If we restrict ourselves to the most recent contributions on this problem, Antonius H. J. Gunneweg and Josef Schreiner have assessed the penitential prayer (1:15–2:35 [3:8]), the wisdom admonition (3:9–4:4), and the salvation oracle (4:5–5:9) to be originally independent units, and the present book to be a secondary composition. Conversely, for composition and tradition-historical or rhetorical reasons, respectively, Odil Hannes Steck and André Kabasele Mukenge have argued for the basic unity of the book. Nevertheless, an understanding of the composite character of the booklet may still be held if one concedes that even redactors can produce sensibly arranged compositions.

Issue 2: The Literary Problem of the Book. A. H. J. Gunneweg, C. A. Moore, and J. Schreiner have based their thesis that the book is a secondary composition on the argument that its three parts vary significantly in terms of theme and content. They proceed from the assumption that 1:15–2:35 was only secondarily linked to 3:9–4:4 by means of 3:1–8 and the observation that the two parts of the penitential prayer also distinguish themselves from one another in terms of diction.[10] In addition, Schreiner points out that 3:10 and 12 have a similar function in linking 3:9–4:4 with 1:15–35, and 4:3–4 in linking 3:9–4:4 with 4:5–5:9, and that the situation presumed in 4:5–5:9 agrees with that presumed in 1:15–35.[11] On the other hand, one who is convinced that the book was well planned will be inclined to attribute these linking texts to the author of the book rather than to its redactor.

Nevertheless, five additional observations can be made in favor of understanding the book as a composite work:

1. As already mentioned above, a contradiction exists concerning the condition of the temple: 1:10–14 assumes that it still exists, 2:26 that it lies in ruins.

2. It seems peculiar that the penitential prayer in 1:15–3:8 is introduced not as the prayer of the Babylonian Jews, but as one they prayed on behalf of the Judeans and Jerusalemites.

---

[10] See A. H. J. Gunneweg, "Das Buch Baruch," in *JSHRZ* 3.2, 168–69; Moore, AB 44, 258–61; and J. Schreiner, "Baruch," in *Klagelieder, Baruch* (ed. H. Groß and J. Schreiner; NEchtB 14; Würzburg: Echter, 1986), 45.

[11] Schreiner, "Baruch."

3. The tenor, corresponding to Jer 29:7, in 1:11–12 with its call to inter-
cede for the Babylonian king contradicts the word of comfort for Jerusalem in 4:31–35 that threatens her enemies with a horrible end.

4. A peculiar overlap in content between 3:36–5:4 and 5:5–9 gives rise
to the notion that Zion's consolation speech and the promise of
consolation addressed to her (4:9b–5:4) were secondarily connected to the preceding by the linking text 4:5–9 and framed by the
dramatic conclusion in 5:5–9.

5. It is surprising that an oracle addressed to Jerusalem follows a
speech placed in Zion's mouth. This alternation may, nonetheless,
be explained by means of the dependence of the personification of
daughter Zion on Lamentations and the compositional intention
of the author of the book.

Consequently, it seems likely that the author of the book could utilize
texts already in existence in his composition, as seems to be the case for the
books of Qoheleth and Sirach.[12] The third observation above attests to the
fact that the texts do not all stem from the same time. The compatibility in
1:18–5:9 and the thoroughgoing integration of the various biblical traditions throughout this section speak for the fact that they originated in a
common institutional or social context. Still, the various opinions concerning the genesis of the book may continue in currency without
diminishing its theological significance.

Thesis 4: Origin and Age. The literary nature of the book as dramatic literature complicates dating, especially if one must also distinguish between
portions that have been appropriated from preexisting materials and the
whole. In both cases, dating can only be based on tradition-historical and
ideological-critical observations. The fictive situation of the whole book,
which assumes a high priest officiating in the Jerusalem temple and a
worldwide Diaspora, corresponds essentially to the condition of Judaism
since the reconstruction of the temple in 520–515 B.C.E. Yet the pseudepigraphical and ahistorical character of the introduction described above

---

[12] See A. A. Fischer, *Skepsis oder Furcht Gottes* (BZAW 248; New York: de Gruyter,
1997), 35–50. In the book of Sirach, the example of Sir 24 illustrates that vv. 24– 29, 30–34
have been appended to wisdom's self-praise by v. 23. On the problem, see also L. Schrader,
Leiden und Gerechtigkeit: Studien zu Theologie und Textgeschichte des Sirachbuches (BBET
27; New York: Lang, 1994), 58–95, who sees the book as the result of unstructured redaction of extant texts; and, to the contrary, J. Föck, "Structure and Redaction History of the
Book of Ben Sira: Review and Prospects," in *The Book of Ben Sira in Modern Research* (ed. P.
C. Beentjes; BZAW 255; New York: de Gruyter, 1997), 61–79, who argues (76–77) that
Sirach himself composed the book gradually and intentionally.

and traditio-historical evidence speak against dating the book before the second century; the absence of literary allusions speak against a dating in the late second and absolutely against the first century B.C.E.;[13] and the content speaks for focusing on the time between 168 and 138 B.C.E. and for origins in Jerusalem.

Issue 3: Age and Provenance. In terms of content, the concentration of the book on Jerusalem suggests that it also originated there. Among possible occasions for its composition, various situations between the religion edict of Antiochus IV Epiphanes (169 B.C.E.) and the destruction of the second temple (70 C.E.) are possible. Accordingly, dates vary between the middle of the second century B.C.E. and the first century C.E. Tradition-critical indices reveal unequivocally that the book can only have originated after Jesus ben Sira. Since the book of Baruch, like 1 Maccabees, takes no notice of apocalyptic expectations such as characterize, for example, the anthology of the *Psalms of Solomon*[14] (completed in the second half of the first century) and the Wisdom of Solomon[15] (from the time of Augustus), a date for the book in the second century B.C.E. seems best. With its threat against the enemies, 4:30–35 may establish the *terminus post* and *ad quem* simultaneously, despite the traditional character of the statement. Presumably, the text responds to a contemporary threat against Jerusalem by a Seleucid ruler. Of these, Antiochus IV Epiphanes (168) was the first to attack Jerusalem in the second century, and Antiochus VII Sidetes (139), the last. Thus, we essentially follow the dating by O. H. Steck[16] and A. Kabasele Mukenge,[17] who commit unequivocally to the time of the high priest Alcimus, however.

Issue 4: The Tradition-critical Backgrounds. In terms of content, 1:15–2:35 reveals itself in vv. 15–20 to be dependent on the prayer in Dan 9:4–19 (compare also 1:16–18 with Dan 9:1–11) and in vv. 21–35 on Deuteronomy and the book of Jeremiah.[18] Since the origin of the prayer in Daniel 9

---

[13] Moore, AB 44, 256, who, therefore, dates the composition before Antiochus IV.

[14] See below, p. 78.

[15] See below, p. 104.

[16] See Steck's extensive comments in *Baruchbuch*, 290–303; and, concisely, in ATD 5, 23.

[17] A. Kabasele Mukenge, *L' unité littéraire du livre de Baruch* (EBib NS 38; Paris: Gabalda, 1998); cited following M. A. Knibb, *SOTS Book List 1999* (Sheffield: Sheffield Academic Press, 1999), 175–76.

[18] See Moore, AB 44, 258–61; and recently, the extensive treatment by O. H. Steck, *Baruchbuch*, 81–115, who, however, regards all portions of the book, except for 3:38 (which he judges to be a Christian interpolation), as has having been composed for their current context from the outset.

is disputed,[19] the absence of a resurrection hope in Bar 2:17 might permit one to infer a pre-Maccabean origin for 1:15–2:35, although, in view of the theology of 1 Maccabees, which also omits it, this argument has no probative force.

The wisdom admonition in 3:9–4:4 calls Israel to obedience to the law as the condition for obtaining salvation. Alongside allusions to the Trito-Isaianic collection, to the book of Job, as well as to the Deuteronomistic theology of history, the concept of the hidden divine wisdom in which Israel participates through the Torah is noteworthy here. It has its closest parallel in Sir 1:1–10 and Sir 24, so that the song is younger than the book of Sirach, composed after 195 and before 175.[20] The small cycle of songs of lament and comfort in 4:5–5:9 consists of a word of comfort to Israel in 4:5–8 that 4:9a links to Jerusalem's lament and her word of comfort and admonition to her exiled children in 4:9b–20 or 4:21–29.[21] The personification of Jerusalem lamenting derives from Lamentations, although the influence of Lamentations is not limited to the allocation of roles.[22] In a similar fashion, the composition, with its sequence of admonition and promise, corresponds to Jeremiah 32. A word of comfort to Jerusalem, styled as divine speech, follows in 4:30–35. It threatens with eternal destruction all cities that have oppressed or abducted her children.[23] Thereby, 4:5–5:9 reveals its relationship with Lamentations in a manner contrasting with its relation to late Deuteronomic scholastic traditions and to Deutero- and Trito-Isaianic salvation oracles.[24] The summons in 5:5–9, addressed to Jerusalem, to take note of the movement of her children dispersed throughout the world, whom God brings on a level road and through shady glens, has a remarkable parallel in *Pss. Sol.* 11:2–6.[25] Nevertheless, it is not certain that this is a case of dependence in one direction or the other,[26] because all the motifs pertinent to the situation

---

[19] See H. Graf Reventlow, *Gebet im Alten Testament* (Stuttgart: Kohlhammer, 1986), 281–82.

[20] For the literary dependencies, see Steck, *Baruchbuch*, 129–39.

[21] For the literary relationships, see Steck, *Baruchbuch*, 187–200, who, however, considers them to be unified (200–203).

[22] See the data in Steck, *Baruchbuch*, 196–97.

[23] Compare, for example, 4:30 with Isa 43:1; 4:35 with Isa 34:9–10, 34; 4:37 with Isa 49:18; 60:4.

[24] Steck, *Baruchbuch*, 187–200.

[25] Compare, for example, Bar 5:1–2 with *Pss. Sol.* 11:7 and Isa 52:1; Bar 5:5 with *Pss. Sol.* 11:2 and Isa 40:11 as the common reference; Bar 5:7 with Isa 40:4–5 and *Pss. Sol.* 11:4; Bar 5:8 with *Pss. Sol.* 11:5 and Isa 41:14–17; and Bar 5:9 with *Pss. Sol.* 11:3a and Isa 35:10 = 52:11.

[26] W. Pesch ("Die Abhängigkeit des 11. salomonischen Psalms vom letzten Kapitel des Buches Baruch," *ZAW* 67 [1955]: 251–52) argued for the dependence of *Pss. Sol.* 11 on Bar 4:36–5:9; C. A. Moore ("Towards the Dating of the Book of Baruch," *CBQ* 36 [1974]: 312–20; and AB 44, 315) argued the converse.

addressed in both texts can be found in the book of Isaiah. If one considers dependence an option, then Bar 5:1–9 must be original as the poetically clearer and theologically weightier exemplar.

Nonetheless, the significant reasons named above contradict such a late dating for the book of Baruch. Consequently, O. H. Steck's suggestion—that the author of the book (and, in our view, also the author of the texts he edited) circulated among the Jerusalem scribes who stand in the tradition of the late redactions of the biblical books—deserves assent.[27]

Issue 5: The Original Language of the Book. As C. J. Ball[28] has already shown through lexical analysis, and recent studies by E. Tov,[29] D. G. Burke,[30] and O. H. Steck[31] have confirmed, vocabulary, syntax, and style reveal that 1:1–3:8 represents a translation from the Hebrew. The same can be postulated also for 3:9–4:4 and even more clearly for 4:5–5:9 on the basis of Semitisms that sometimes amount to mistranslations. Occasional agreements with the Septuagint text in obvious or subtle biblical citations can be explained as the result of the fact that the translator also had access to texts similar to the Septuagint.[32]

Issue 6: Witnesses to the Text. Fragments of the booklet have been discovered at Qumran and in the desert of Judea. In addition to the Greek version, it is extant in three Latin versions, one of which Jerome adopted for the Vulgate. It is further transmitted in Syriac in the Peshitta and the Syro-Hexapla, in Coptic, and in Ethiopic. This circumstance reflects its status in the early church, which, in accord with the book's placement following Jeremiah, often cited its words as Jeremianic. Because Baruch was understood as a prediction of the incarnation of divine wisdom in Jesus Christ, 3:38 enjoyed special popularity. Yet this verse is often, if not conclusively, judged a Christian insertion.[33]

Thesis 5: The Intention of the Book. The book of Baruch serves to revitalize hope for liberation from Seleucid domination and for the return of the worldwide Diaspora to Zion by God, who has mercy on his people. It is

---

[27] Steck, *Baruchbuch,* 306–11; or (concisely) GAT 24.

[28] C. J. Ball, *APOT* 1:597.

[29] E. Tov, *The Septuagint Translation of Jeremiah and Baruch: A Discussion of an Early Revision of the LXX of Jeremiah 29–52 and Baruch 1:1–3:8* (HSM 8; Missoula: Scholars Press, 1976).

[30] D. G. Burke, *The Poetry of Baruch* (SBLSCS 11; Chico: Scholars Press, 1982).

[31] Steck, *Baruchbuch,* 249–53.

[32] See Steck, *Baruchbuch,* 139 and 203–4.

[33] With Gunneweg, "Buch Baruch," 177; compare Sir 24:10–13 and Wis 9:10.

thus a call to penitence and obedience to the divine commandments as the condition of redemption (2:27–35; 3:9; 4:1–2).

Bibliography

Introduction:
Oesterley. *Introduction*, 256–67.
Eißfeldt. *Introduction*, 592–94.
Rost. *EinlApo*, 50–53.
Schürer/Vermes 3.1:733–43.
H.-P. Rüger. "Apokryphen I.12," *TRE* 3:307.
I. Meyer, "Das Buch Baruch und der Brief des Jeremia," in Zenger, *Einleitung*, 435–39.

Issues:
W. Pesch. "Die Abhängigkeit des 11. salomonischen Psalms vom letzten Kapitel des Buches Baruch." *ZAW* 67 (1955): 251–63.
B. N. Wambacq. "Les prières de Baruch (I,15–II,19) et Daniel (IX,5–19)." *Bib* 40 (1959): 463–75.
———. "L'unité littéraire de Baruch 1,1–3,8." Pages 455–60 in *Sacra Pagina: Miscellanea Biblica Congressus Internationalis de Re Biblica*. Edited by J. Coppens et al. BETL 12. Gembloux: Duculot, 1959.
———. "L'unité du livre de Baruch." *Bib* 47 (1966): 547–76.
E. Haenchen. "Das Buch Baruch." Pages 299–334 in *Gott und Mensch: Gesammelte Aufsätze*. Edited by Ernst Haenchen. Tübingen: Mohr, 1965.
C. A. Moore. "Towards the Dating of the Book of Baruch." *CBQ* 36 (1974): 312–20.
E. Tov. *The Septuagint Translation of Jeremiah and Baruch: A Discussion of an Early Revision of the LXX of Jeremiah 29–52 and Baruch 1:1–3:8*. HSM 8. Missoula: Scholars Press, 1976.
J. A. Goldstein. "The Apocryphal Book of Baruch." *PAAJR* 46/47 (1979/1980): 179–99.
P.-M. Bogaert. "Le personnage de Baruch et l'histoire du livre de Jérémie: Aux origines du livre deutérocanonique de Baruch." Pages 73–81 in *Papers Presented to the Fifth International Congress on Biblical Studies Held at Oxford, 1973*. Edited by E. A. Livingstone. Studia evangelica 7/TU 126. Berlin: Akademie Verlag, 1982.
D. G. Burke. *The Poetry of Baruch*. SBLSCS 11. Chico: Scholars Press, 1982.
O. H. Steck. *Das apokryphe Baruchbuch: Studien zu Rezeption und Konzentration "kanonischer" Überlieferung*. FRLANT 160. Göttingen: Vandenhoeck & Ruprecht, 1993.

————. "Israels Gott statt anderer Götter—Israels Gesetz statt fremder Weisheit: Beobachtungen zur Rezeption von Hi 28 in Bar 3,9–4,4." Pages 457–71 in *"Wer ist wie du, HERR, unter den Göttern?": Studien zur Theologie und Religionsgechichte Israel: Für Otto Kaiser zum 70. Geburtstag.* Edited by I. Kottsieper et al. Göttingen: Vandenhoeck & Ruprecht, 1994.

A. Kabasele Mukenge. *L'unité littéraire du livre de Baruch.* EBib NS 38. Paris: Gabalda, 1998.

Commentaries:
J. Rothstein, *APAT,* 1900; O. C. Whitehouse, *APOT,* 1913; E. Kalt, HSAT, 1932; V. Hamp, EB, 1958[4]; B. Wambacq, BDT, 1957; A. H. J. Gunneweg, *JSHRZ,* 1975; J. Schreiner, NEchtB, 1986; O. H. Steck, GAT, 1998.

The Letter of Jeremiah

Thesis: The seventy-two verses of the Letter of Jeremiah (Ep Jer) comprise a pseudepigraphical pamphlet concerning the groundlessness of fear of idols, equated with their images.[34] Its polemic depends on the pertinent Old Testament texts.[35] It is based on a Hebrew or Aramaic original and was already distributed in Greek in first-century B.C.E. Palestine. As was already the case in the younger Septuagint manuscripts, it is counted as the sixth chapter of the book of Baruch in the Old Latin and, following it, in the Vulgate and the newer translations of the Bible. It presumably originated in the early Hellenistic period.

Issue 1: Literary Character and Content of the Document. In its superscription, the booklet identifies itself as a copy of a letter that the prophet Jeremiah sent to those destined for deportation. In terms of its literary character, however, it represents instructional literature concerning the invalidity of the gods (whom it identifies with their images). It opens with an introduction in vv. 1–6 that predicts the encounter of those destined for deportation with idol processions and that challenges them not to fear the idols but to worship the Lord. Subsequently, ten sections treat the theme of the invalidity of the gods, again identified with their images, and of the deceit perpetrated with them. The first nine[36] conclude with a refrain, and the tenth (vv. 69–72) summarizes the assessment of their invalidity. The principle arguments against idols are the process of their

---

[34] See R. G. Kratz, ATD 5, 84–87.
[35] Compare the summary in Moore, AB 44, 319–23.
[36] Vv. 7–14, 15–22, 23–28, 29–39, 40–44, 45–51, 52–56, 57–64, 65–68.

production, their immobility, helplessness, and need for maintenance, and, finally, their inability to intervene in the history of an individual's life. By means of the fictional dress of his document, the author recalls Jeremiah 29. Above all, Deut 4:27–28; Isa 44:9–20, 46:7–8; Jer 10:1–16; and Ps 115:4–8, 135:15–18 prompt his polemic against idol images.

Issue 2: Age and Provenance of the Document. The prediction made in v. 2 to the deportees concerning a stay in Babylon lasting up to seven generations, and thus far surpassing the seventy years of Jer 29:10, offers a starting point. Whether one reckons the 280 years to begin in 597 or 587 or considers the number merely symbolic, the letter must date at least to the early Hellenistic period. The Greek papyrus fragment 7Q2 from the first century B.C.E. constitutes the *terminus ad quem.* In the event that *Jub.* 11–12 and 2 Macc 2:2 have the Letter of Jeremiah in view (which is at least likely), the lowest limit for the origin of the letter would be the middle or the end of the second century B.C.E.,[37] although the origin of the Greek translation could lie closer to an early date. Thus, C. A. Moore proposes the end of the fourth century,[38] J. Schreiner more precisely the time of Alexander the Great,[39] and R. G. Kratz that of Antiochus III[40] who explicitly promoted the cult of the Babylonian gods. In any case, the booklet serves to immunize Diaspora Jewry, presumably especially the Babylonian *golah,* against the worship of pagan idol images. The author might have known the cult of foreign gods not only from the literature but also by personal experience. Yet it remains more probable[41] that he obtained his information indirectly and worked in Palestine.[42] His rationalistic idol-and-cult polemic attests his proximity to wisdom tradition, and his knowledge of Scripture his membership in scribal circles. Therefore, he probably lived among priestly or Levitical scribes.

Issue 3: The Attestation and Original Language of the Document. The Letter of Jeremiah survives only in Greek or in translations dependent on the Septuagint. The oldest manuscript evidence is the Greek papyrus fragment 7Q2 from the first century B.C.E.[43] Since the author of the letter relies

---

[37] See K. Berger, *Das Buch der Jubiläen* (*JSHRZ* 2.3; Gütersloh: Mohn, 1981), 299–300.

[38] Moore, AB 44, 328.

[39] J. Schreiner, NEchtB 49.

[40] Kratz, ATD 5, 83–84.

[41] See Moore, AB 44, 328–29.

[42] Kratz, ATD 5, 24.

[43] See M. Baillet, J. T. Milik, and R. de Vaux (with a contribution by H. W. Baker), *Les "petites grottes" de Qumran* (DJD 3; Oxford: Clarendon, 1962), 143 and pl. xxx, with the sigla 7Q2 (LXX EpJer).

on the text of M instead of G for his rendition of Jer 10:5, the Greek version contains a series of Semitisms, and a few of its unusual phrases are to be explained as translation errors,[44] the most likely conclusion seems to be that the book was originally composed in Hebrew or Aramaic.[45]

Bibliography

Introduction:
Oesterley. *Introduction*, 268–71.
Eißfeldt. *Introduction*, 594–95.
Rost. *EinlApo*, 53–54.
H.-P. Rüger. "Apokryphen I.13," *TRE* 3:308–16.
Schürer/Vermes 3.2:743–45.
I. Meyer. "Der Brief des Jeremia," in Zenger, *Einleitung*, 439–40.

The Issues:
W. Naumann. *Untersuchungen über den apokryphen Jeremiabrief.* BZAW
    25. Gießen: Töpelmann, 1913.
E. S. Artom. "Il origine, la data e gli scopi dell' Epistola di Geremia."
    Annuario studi ebraici 1 (1935): 49–74.
D. Kellermann. "Apokryphes Obst. Bemerkungen zur Epistula Jeremiae
    (Baruch Kap.6), insbesondere zu Vers 42." *ZDMG* 129 (1979): 23–42.
R. G. Kratz. "Die Rezeption von Jer. 10 und 29 im pseudepigraphen Brief
    des Jeremia." *JSJ* 26 (1995): 1–31.

Commentaries:
J. Rothstein, *APAT,* 1900; C. J. Ball, *APOT,* 1912; E. Kalt, HSAT, 1932; B.
Wambacq, BOT, 1957; V. Hamp, EB, 1958[4]; A. H. J. Gunneweg, *JSHRZ,*
1975 (1980); C. A. Moore, AB, 1977; J. Schreiner, NEchtB, 1986; R. Kratz,
ATD, 1998.

The Apocalyptic Literature

Thesis 1: The Character of Judeo-apocalyptic Literature. The pseudonymous
Jewish writings categorized as apocalypses or revelations employ a narrative

---

[44] Compare, for example, vv. 10, 15, 30, and 71 following Gunneweg, "Buch Baruch,"
185–86; and, especially, D. Kellermann, "Apokryphen Obst. Bemerkungen zur Epistula
Jeremiae (Baruch Kap. 6), insbesonder zu Vers 42," *ZDMG* 129 (1979): 23–42.

[45] So, most recently, Kratz, ATD 5, 18.

framework to unfold secret eschatological knowledge concerning the end of current history, the beginning of the kingdom of God, and the future of the dead. For this knowledge, they appeal to a supernatural mediation by a figure from antiquity.[46]

Issue 1: Apocalyptic Literature. The genre has precursors in prophetic literature and, especially, the night visions of the book of Zechariah.[47] Following the crystallization of the tradition in the third century B.C.E., independent Jewish apocalyptic literature begins with the Book of the Watchers (that is, the ever wakeful throne angels), *1 Enoch* 1–36,[48] to reach its apex between the second century B.C.E. and the second century

---

[46] Compare the explication of the concept by J. J. Collins ("Towards the Morphology of a Genre," *Semeia* 14 [1970]: 9, cited in Collins, *Daniel*, 4): "Apocalypse is a genre of revelatory literature with a narrative framework, in which a revelation is mediated by an otherworldly being to a human recipient, disclosing a transcendent reality which is both temporal, insofar as it envisages eschatological salvation, and spatial insofar as it involves another, supernatural world." See also H. Stegemann, "Die Bedeutung der Qumranfunde für die Apokalyptik," in *Apocalypticism in the Mediterranean World and the Near East: Proceedings of the International Colloquium on Apocalypticism, Uppsala, August 12–17, 1979* (ed. D. Hellholm; 2d ed.; Tübingen: Mohr, 1989), 495–530; and J. J. Collins, "The Genre Apocalypse in Hellenistic Judaism," in *Apocalypticism in the Mediterranean World*, 531–48; Collins, *The Apocalyptic Imagination: An Introduction to Jewish Apocalyptic Literature* (2d ed.; Grand Rapids: Eerdmans, 1998), 2–5; and regarding the controversy surrounding the definition, see D. S. Russell, *Divine Disclosure: An Introduction to Jewish Apocalyptic* (Minneapolis: Fortress, 1992), 8–10, who appropriately distinguishes between apocalypse as a literary genre, apocalypticism as a complex of religious concepts, and apocalyptic eschatology as the ideas concerning the last things contained in the pertinent literature. Regarding the religio-historical background of the rise of apocalypticism, compare the still useful M. Hengel, *Judaism and Hellenism* (Philadelphia: Fortress, 1974), 175–21 (the Hasidim and the initial apex of Jewish apocalypticism) and 210–18 (wisdom through revelation).

[47] See H. Gese, "Anfang und Ende der Apokalyptik, dargestellt am Sacharjabuch," *ZTK* 70 (1973): 20–49 (= Gese, *Vom Sinai zum Zion: Alttestamentliche Beiträge zur biblischen Theologie* [3d ed.; BEvT 64; Munich: Kaiser, 1989], 202–30); and, in contrast, P. D. Hanson, *The Dawn of Apocalyptic: The Historical and Sociological Roots of Jewish Apocalyptic Eschatology* (2d ed.; Philadelphia: Fortress, 1979), 253–56.

[48] See the treatment by G. Beer, *APAT* 2:236–57; *APOT* 2:188–208; E. Isaac, *OTP* 1:13–37; S. Uhlig, *JSHRZ* 5.6, 506–72; and M. Black, *The Book of Enoch or I Enoch: A New English Edition with Commentary and Textual Notes, with an Appendix on the "Astronomical" Chapters (72–82) by O. Neugebauer* (SVTP 7; Leiden: Brill, 1985), 25–42, in addition to the commentary (103–81); compare J. T. Milik and M. Black, eds. *The Books of Enoch: Aramaic Fragments of Qumrân Cave 4* (Oxford: Clarendon 1976); the Aramaic fragments in text and translation by K. Beyer, *Die Texte vom Toten Meer* (Göttingen: Vandenhoeck & Ruprecht, 1984), 225–43; regarding the literary problems of the book, see especially, F. García Martínez, *Qumran and Apocalyptic: Studies on the Aramaic Texts from Qumran* (STDJ 9; Leiden: Brill, 1993); regarding the *Book of Noah* utilized in the Book of the Watchers, see *Qumran and Apocalyptic*, 26–36; and on the whole book, A.-M. Denis, *Introduction aux pseudépigraphes grecs d'Ancien Testament* (SVTP 1; Leiden: Brill, 1970), 15–30; and Schürer/Vermes 3.1:250–68 (with bibliography).

C.E.[49] As a rule, figures from antiquity such as Enoch (Gen 5:21–24), Noah, Moses, Baruch, and Ezra appear in Jewish apocalypses as fictive receivers of revelation. (In contrast, standing in the tradition of Jewish apocalypticism, the author of the Revelation of John, otherwise considered the model for the entirety of the pertinent literature, often identifies himself by his own name [Rev 1:1, 4, 9; 22:8].)[50]

Thesis 2: The Types of Apocalypses. One can distinguish fundamentally between apocalypses with revelations in world history and those with supernatural journeys.

Issue 2: The Types of Apocalypses. Besides the book of Daniel, the historical apocalypses include the Book of Visions (*1 Enoch* 83–91*),[51] the Letter of Enoch (*1 Enoch* 91–107*) with the Apocalypse of the Ten Weeks (*1 Enoch* 93:1–10; 91:11–17),[52] Jubilees,[53] *4 Ezra*,[54] and the Syriac *Apocalypse of*

---

[49] Compare, now, especially the comprehensive portrayal by Collins, *Apocalyptic Imagination,* which treats even the pertinent early Christian documents; or, for quick and comprehensive information, the article "Apokalyptik/Apokalypsen," *TRE* 3:189–289, with contributions by G. Lanczkowski (religio-historical); J. Lebram (Old Testament) ; Kh. Müller (Judaism); A. Strobel (New Testament); K. H. Schwarte (early church); K.-H. R. Konrad (Middle Ages); D. Seebaß (Reformation and early modern).

[50] See P. Vielhauer, *Geschichte der urchristlichen Literatur: Einleitung in das Neue Testament, die Apokrypha und den Apostolischen Vätern* (GL; New York: de Gruyter, 1975), 502; or E. Lohse, *Die Entstehung des Neuen Testaments* (5th ed.; ThW 4; Stuttgart: Kohlhammer, 1991), 144.

[51] See the treatments by Beer, *APAT* 2:288–98; *APOT* 2:248–60; Isaac, *OTP* 1:61–72; and Uhlig, *JSHRZ* 5.6, 673–707.

[52] See the treatments by Beer, *APAT* 2:298–308; *APOT* 60–77; Isaac, *OTP* 1:72–86; Uhlig, *JSHRZ* 5.6, 72–74; and Black, *Book of Enoch,* 71–83, 254–80; regarding the literary problems, see García Martínez, *Qumran und Apocalyptic,* 79–96, for the discussion of the Apocalypse of Weeks and whether it belongs to the Letter of Enoch, 79–93; regarding the specific critique of F. Dexinger, *Henochs Zehnwochenapokalypse und offene Probleme der Apokalyptikforschung* (StPB 29; Leiden: Brill, 1977), see J. C. Vanderkam, "Studies in the Apocalypse of Weeks (1 Enoch 93,1–10; 91,11–17)," *CBQ* 46 (1984): 511–23.

[53] See the treatments by E. Littmann, *APAT* 2:31–110; *APOT* 2:1–82; O. S. Wintermute, *OTP* 2:35–142; regarding the literary problems, see Denis, *Introduction,* 150–62; and Schürer/Vermes 3.1:308–18 (with bibliography).

[54] See the treatments by H. Gunkel, *APAT* 2:331–401; G. H. Box, *APOT* 2:542–642; J. Schreiner, *JSHRZ* 5.4 (with bibliography); B. M. Metzger, *OTP* 1:517–60; on the theology, see W. Harnisch, *Verhängnis und Verheißung der Geschichte: Untersuchungen zum Zeit- und Geschichtsverständnis im 4. Buch Esra und in der syr. Baruchapokalypse* (FRLANT 97; Göttingen: Vandenhoeck & Ruprecht, 1969); Harnisch, "Der Prophet als Widerpart und Zeuge der Offenbarung: Erwägungen zur Interdependenz von Form und Sache im IV Buch Esra," in *Apocalypticism in the Mediterranean World,* 461–93; E. Brandenburger, *Die Verborgenheit Gottes im Weltgeschehen: Das literarische und theologische Problem des 4. Esrabuches* (ATANT 68; Zurich: Theologische Verlag Zürich, 1981); regarding the literary problems, see Denis, *Introduction,* 194–200; and Schürer/Vermes 3.1:294–307.

Baruch (2 Baruch).[55] The apocalypses with journeys to heaven and the underworld include the Book of the Watchers (*1 Enoch* 1–36),[56] the Astronomical Book (*1 Enoch* 72–82),[57] the Parables (*1 Enoch* 37–71),[58] Slavonic or *2 Enoch,*[59] the Greek *Apocalypse of Baruch (3 Baruch),*[60] the *Testament of Levi* 2–5,[61] and the *Apocalypse of Abraham,* for example.[62]

Issue 3: Genres Encountered in the Apocalypses.[63] Symbolic dreams (compare, for example, Dan 2 and 4 or Dan 7 and 8; *1 Enoch* 83–84; *4 Ezra* 11–12; *2 Bar.* 35–47), visions with the appearance of a heavenly being (compare, for example, Dan 10), communications from an angel (compare Dan 11; *Jub.* 2:1–3), and revelation dialogues (compare, for example, *4 Ezra* 4:1–11:34; *2 Bar.* 1:1–5:4) appear as means of secret revelation. The communications can ensue in a revelation dialogue in the form of an exegetical midrash (Dan 9). *Jubilees* can be categorized as a narrative midrash. Pesher, an interpretation or commentary (compare, for example, Dan 2:3–7, 24–45; 4:3–4; 5:7–8, 15–28; 1QpHab; 4QpNah; 4QpPs 37),

[55] See V. Ryssel, *APAT* 2:402–45; R. H. Charles, *APOT* 2:470–526; F. J. Klijn, *JSHRZ* 5.2, 103–85; Klijn, *OTP* 1:615–20; regarding the theology, see Harnisch, *Verhängnis;* regarding the literary problems, see Schürer/Vermes 3.2:750–56 (with bibliography).

[56] Compare n. 48, above.

[57] See the treatments by Beer, *APAT* 2:78–87; *APOT* 2:237–48; Isaac, *OTP* 1:50–61; Uhlig, *JSHRZ* 5.6, 635–72; and O. Neugebauer, "'Astronomical' Chapters," in *Book of Enoch,* 386–419; regarding astronomy and theology, see M. Albani, *Astronomie und Schöpfungsglaube: Untersuchungen zum astronomischen Henochbuch* (WMANT 68; Neukirchen-Vluyn: Neukirchener Verlag, 1996).

[58] See the treatments by Beer, *APAT* 58–78; *APOT* 2:208–32; Isaac, *OTP,* 28–50; and Uhlig, *JSHRZ* 5.6, 258–78; regarding the literary problems, see Schürer/Vermes 3.1:256–59; and García Martínez, *Qumran and Apocalyptic,* 21–23.

[59] See the treatments in *APOT* 2:470–526; F. I. Andersen, *OTP* 1:91–221; and C. Böttrich, *JSHRZ* 5.7, 777–1040 (with bibliography); regarding the literary problems, see E. Turdeanu, *Apocryphes slaves et roumaines de l'Ancien Testament* (SVTP 5; Leiden: Brill, 1981), 364–91; and Schürer/Vermes 3.2:746–56.

[60] See the treatments by V. Ryssel, *APAT* 2:446–57; H. M. Hughes, *APOT* 2:527–41; E. Gaylord, *OTP* 1:653–80; and U. B. Müller, *JSHRZ* 5.2, 85–102; regarding the literary problems, see Denis, *Introduction,* 79–84; D. H. Harlow, *The Greek Apocalypse of Baruch (3 Baruch) in Hellenistic Judaism and Early Christianity* (SVTP 12; Leiden: Brill, 1996), and Schürer/Vermes 3.2:789–93.

[61] See the treatments by F. Schnapp, *APAT* 2:465–78; R. H. Charles, *APOT* 2:304–15; H. C. Kee, *OTP* 1:788–85; H. W. Hollander and M. de Jonge, *The Testaments of the Twelve Patriarchs: A Commentary* (SVTP 8; Leiden: Brill, 1985), 129–83; regarding the Aramaic fragments from Qumran, 1Q21 and 4Q213 and 214, see Beyer, *Texte,* 188–209; regarding the literary problems of the *Testament of the Twelve Patriarchs,* see Schürer/Vermes 3.2:767–81.

[62] See the treatments by B. Philonenko-Sayar and M. Philonenko, *JSHRZ* 5.5, 409–60; and R. Rubinkiewicz, *OTP* 1:681–706; regarding the literary problems, see also Schürer/Vermes 3.1:288–92.

[63] See Collins, *Daniel,* 6–11; or Collins, *Apocalyptic Imagination,* 1–42.

which, in contrast to the midrash, explicates individual statements or phrases, is related to exegetical midrash.[64] Finally, there is the revelation report in which the recipient of revelation communicates the content of the received revelation (compare the Ten Week Apocalypse, *1 Enoch* 93:1–10; 91:12–19).

Issue 4: Ethiopic or 1 Enoch. Because of its particular significance for the history of Jewish apocalypticism from the third century B.C.E. to at least the first century C.E., an overview of the individual sections of *1 Enoch* follows. Since its complete text is only preserved in Ethiopic, it is also designated Ethiopic *Enoch*[65] although it represents a translation of the Greek *Enoch.* The Greek is, however, only partially preserved.[66] In turn, this translation is based on the Aramaic original of which a sufficient number of fragments have been found in Cave 4 at Qumran to sharpen the picture of the origin of the book.[67] (Indeed, the texts discovered in the caves at Qumran have also enriched the portrayal of Jewish eschatology in general.)[68] *First Enoch* contains the following originally independent documents: (1) the Book of the Watchers (*1 Enoch* 1–36); (2) the Parables (*1 Enoch* 37–71); (3) the Astronomical Book (*1 Enoch* 72–82); (4) the Dreams including the Animal Apocalypse (*1 Enoch* 83–90); and (5) the Letter of Enoch including the Apocalypse of Weeks (*1 Enoch* 91–105). There follows the appendices: in *1 Enoch* 106–107, the fragment of a Noah apocalypse, and in *1 Enoch* 108, Enoch's admonition to his son, Methuselah, and to his descendents in the end time who observe the law.

Issue 5: The Age and Significance of the Books Contained in 1 Enoch.[69] Based on the fragmentary manuscript discoveries from Qumran Cave 4, the age of the individual portions may be determined as follows: The Astronomical Book (72–82), originating in the third century B.C.E., is the oldest of these documents. It was originally transmitted independently and may have replaced the Book of the Giants when it was incorporated into the *Enoch* corpus. This work is attested in its original form only through the

---

[64] See M. P. Horgan, *Pesharim: Qumran Interpretations of Biblical Books* (CBQMS 8; Washington: Catholic Biblical Association of America, 1979).

[65] See the edition by M. A. Knibb and E. Ullendorff (*The Ethiopic Book of Enoch: A New Edition in the Light of the Aramaic Dead Sea Fragments I–II* [Oxford: Clarendon, 1978]), which also takes account of the Aramaic fragments.

[66] See the edition of fragments by M. Black, *Apocalypsis henochi graece* (PVTG 3; Leiden: Brill, 1970).

[67] Milik and Black, *The Books of Enoch.*

[68] See Collins, *Apocalypticism.*

[69] See García Martínez, *Qumran and Apocalyptic,* 113–15.

Aramaic fragments from Qumran Cave 4 and, further, in Middle Persian and Sogdianic Manichean manuscripts that trace back to the translation by Mani.[70] Its content concentrates on the account of the fall of the angels and is thus probably dependent on the portrayal of the conceptually related Enochite Book of the Watchers. Presumably, the two were joined in the first half of the second century B.C.E.[71]

The Book of the Watchers (1–36), the ever-wakeful angels, also belongs to the third century B.C.E. *First Enoch* 6:1–19:3 treats extensively the incomprehensible story from Gen 6:1–4[72] of the fall of the angels and its consequences. We also learn in 6:7, 8:1–2, 10:4–6, and 13:1–2 the identity of Asasel, who, according to Lev 16:10–22, lives in the wilderness as the recipient of the scapegoat, and why he is held captive there.[73] In the two final centuries B.C.E. the fall of the angels had the same significance that has been assigned to the biblical Fall (Gen 3) since the first century C.E.[74] *First Enoch* 9:1 contains the oldest list of the archangels. Their number totals four here. The list in chapter 20 offers instead the names of seven archangels.[75] The most important among them are Michael, Uriel, Gabriel, and Raphael. Michael is the leader of the heavenly hosts (22:16), the angel of judgment who knows the secrets of the end time (10), the mediator between God and humans (1QM 17:7), the dragon slayer (Acts 12:7–9; compare Dan 7, where he is identical with the one "like a human being"), and Israel's champion in the eschatological battle (Dan 12:1).[76] Uriel explores

---

[70] See García Martínez, *Qumran and Apocalyptic*, 106–10.

[71] See L. T. Stuckenbruck, *The Book of Giants from Qumran: Text, Translation and Commentary* (TSAJ 63; Tübingen: Mohr/Siebeck, 1997).

[72] For a literary-critical assessment, see M. Witte, *Die biblische Urgeschichte: Redaktions- und theologiegeschichtliche Beobachtungen zu Genesis 1,1–11,26* (BZAW 265; New York: de Gruyter, 1998), 65–74; for the tradition-historical backgrounds, see 293–97.

[73] See C. Molenberg, "A Study of the Role of Shemihaza and Asasel in Enoch 6–11," *JJS* 35 (1984): 136–46; for a discussion of the religio-historical background of the Old Testament reception of Asasel, see O. Loretz, *Leberschau, Sündenbock, Asasel in Ugarit und Israel* (UBL 3; Altenberge: CIS Verlag, 1985); and B. Janowski, "Azazel und der Sündenbock: Zur Religionsgeschichte von Leviticus 16,10.21f.," in *Gottes Gegenwart in Israel* (ed. B. Janowski; Neukirchen-Vluyn: Neukirchener Verlag, 1993), 285–302.

[74] Regarding the Jewish reception of Gen 6:1–4, see also O. Betz, *Jesus: Aufsätze zur biblischen Theologie II* (WUNT 52; Tübingen: Mohr, 1990), 140–41.

[75] Regarding the hierarchization of the angels as a rationalization consonant with the Hellenistic mind and its religio-historical background, see Hengel, *Judaism and Hellenism*, 231–34; regarding the archangels, see H. Bietenhard, *Die himmlische Welt im Urchristentum und Spätjudentum* (WUNT 2; Tübingen: Mohr, 1951); and M. Mach, *Entwicklungsstadien des jüdischen Engelglaubens in vorrabbinischer Zeit* (STDJ 34; Tübingen: Mohr/Siebeck, 1993); *DDD* 1299–1300.

[76] His name means "Who is like God?" Regarding the many functions attributed to him in Judaism, see *DDD* 1065–72.

the paths of the stars, over whose course he watches (*1 Enoch* 72–82; compare 33:3–4). As such, he belongs to the angels who execute the Last Judgment (*Sib. Or.* 2:215). Later he becomes the interpreting angel.[77] Gabriel is the messenger of the divine will (*1 Enoch* 9:21; Luke 1:19, 26). Together with Michael, Uriel, and Raphael he observes what transpires on earth in order to report it to God (*1 Enoch* 9:1–11).[78] Raphael, however, bears the prayers of the righteous to God, accompanies them on their way, and heals their illnesses (Tob 12:12–15).[79]

In chapter 22 one encounters the first description of the underworld in which the spirits of the dead are assigned to different levels. Of its four (originally three) caves, two are dark. In them one finds the souls of the evildoers. Those who were already punished during their lifetimes remain in the underworld forever, while the others leave at the Last Judgment to go to their sentencing and eternal punishment (compare Dan 12:2). The third cave has a source of illumination. In it the souls of the righteous await their resurrection and translation to heaven. Yet a fourth hell has been secondarily inserted into the text. In it are found the spirit of Abel and all the murdered innocents since. Their lament reminds God to hold judgment for the sinners.[80] The eschatological portrayal finds in chapters 24–27 its further exposition extending to the Last Judgment and the transferral of the tree of life from the mountain of God to Zion.[81]

The Book of Parables (37–71) is not attested at Qumran and, as a whole, is presumably a creation of the first century C.E.[82] On the basis of the content of the Animal Apocalypse, which reaches to the rise of Judas Maccabaeus, the Book of Visions (83–90) is to be dated after his rise but before his death, thus between 165 and 161.

The Apocalypse of Weeks integrated into the Letter of Enoch (91–105) originated between 170 and 165. If it belonged to the letter from the outset, the letter's age is thus determined. It presumes the origin of sin

---

[77] His name may mean "Light" or "Fire of God." See *DDD* 1670–72.

[78] His name probably means "God is my champion." Regarding his tasks, see *DDD* 640–42.

[79] His name means "God has healed." Regarding his tasks, see *DDD* 1299–1300.

[80] See M.-Th. Wacker, *Weltordnung und Gericht: Studien zu 1 Henoch 22* (2d ed.; FB 45; Würzburg: Echter, 1985).

[81] Compare the portrayals of Jewish eschatology in G. W. E. Nickelsburg, *Resurrection, Immortality, and Eternal Life in Intertestamental Judaism* (HTS 26; Cambridge: Harvard University Press, 1971); H. C. C. Cavallin, *Life after Death: Paul's Argument for the Resurrection of the Dead in I Cor 15, Part I: An Enquiry into the Jewish Background* (ConBNT 7/1; Lund: Gleerup, 1974); and U. Fischer, *Eschatologie und Jenseitserwartungen im Hellenistischen Diasporajudentum* (BZNW 44; New York: de Gruyter, 1978).

[82] Regarding it and its significance for extra-Christian speculation concerning the Son of Man, see also Collins, *Apocalyptic Imagination,* 177–93.

through the fall of the angels. The Book of Watchers extensively treats this fall together with its consequences, and the Animal Vision in an astral version alludes to it (compare 88:1–3).[83] Chapters 100–115 are significant for the concepts of the punishment of sinners in fire (100:7–9; compare *1 Enoch* 27 and Isa 66:24) at the Last Judgment and of the transferral of the righteous into the heavenly world (104:1–5; compare Dan 12:3).[84] Finally, an assessment of apocalypticism on the example of the book of *Enoch* would be incomplete if it did not call attention to the fact that the apocalypticists refer to their insight into God's plan for history[85] in order to give their addressees the strength to remain true to their God, since the end of the present era and thus the annihilation of the enemies and the redemption of the dead and living faithful are imminent. The concept of God's plan of history that *Enoch* reveals from beginning to end stands in the service of what we would today call pastoral care.

Bibliography

Sources:

E. Kautzsch, ed. *Die Apokryphen und Pseudepigraphen des Alten Testaments II: Die Pseudepigraphen des Alten Testaments.* Tübingen: Mohr, 1900.

R. H. Charles, ed. *The Apocrypha and Pseudepigrapha of the Old Testament I–II: With Introductions and Critical and Explanatory Notes to the Several Books.* Oxford: Clarendon, 1913.

J. T. Milik and M. Black, eds. *The Books of Enoch: Aramaic Fragments of Qumrân Cave 4.* Oxford: Clarendon 1976.

M. A. Knibb and E. Ullendorff, eds. *The Ethiopic Book of Enoch: A New Edition in the Light of the Aramaic Dead Sea Fragments I–II.* Oxford: Clarendon, 1978.

M. Black. *Apocalypsis henochi graece.* Fragmenta pseudepigraphorum quae supersunt graeca. A.-M. Denis, ed. PVTG 3. Leiden: Brill, 1970.

E. Brandenburger et al. *Jüdisches Schrifttum aus griechisch-römischer Zeit V: Apokalypsen.* Gütersloh: Mohn, 1979ff.

J. H. Charlesworth, ed. *The Old Testament Pseudepigrapha I: Apocalyptic Literature and Testaments.* Garden City, N.Y.: Doubleday, 1983.

---

[83] See also Mach, *Entwicklungsstadien,* 174–76.

[84] For the sociohistorical background, see G. W. E. Nickelsburg, "Social Aspects of Palestinian Jewish Apocalytpicism," in *Apocalypticism in the Mediterranean World,* 641–54.

[85] Regarding the Old Testament roots of the concept, see W. Werner, *Studien zur alttestamentlichen Vorstellung vom Plan Jahwes* (BZAW 173; New York: de Gruyter, 1988), 292–302.

————. *II: Expansions of the "Old Testament" and Legends, Wisdom and Philosophical Literature, Prayers, Psalms, and Odes, Fragments of Lost Judeo-Hellenistic Works.* Garden City, N.Y.: Doubleday, 1988.

K. Beyer. *Die Texte vom Toten Meer.* Göttingen: Vandenhoeck & Ruprecht, 1984.

M. Black. *The Book of Enoch or I Enoch: A New English Edition with Commentary and Textual Notes, with an Appendix on the "Astronomical" Chapters (72–82) by O. Neugebauer.* SVTP 7. Leiden: Brill, 1985.

H. W. Hollander and M. de Jonge. *The Testaments of the Twelve Patriarchs: A Commentary.* SVTP 8. Leiden: Brill, 1985.

L. T. Stuckenbruck. *The Book of Giants from Qumran: Text, Translation and Commentary.* TSAJ 63. Tübingen: Mohr/Siebeck, 1997.

Introduction:
A.-M. Denis. *Introduction aux pseudépigraphes grecs d'Ancien Testament.* SVTP 1. Leiden: Brill, 1970.

Schürer/Vermes 3.1:1–2.

The State of the Discussion:
D. Hellholm, ed. *Apocalypticism in the Mediterranean World and the Near East: Proceedings of the International Colloquium on Apocalypticism, Uppsala, August 12–17, 1979.* 2d ed. Tübingen: Mohr/Siebeck, 1989.

Comprehensive Portrayals:
D. S. Russell. *The Method and Message of Jewish Apocalyptic, 200 B.C.–A.D. 100.* OTL. London: SCM, 1964.

————. *Divine Disclosure: An Introduction to Jewish Apocalyptic.* Minneapolis: Fortress, 1992.

M. Hengel. *Judaism and Hellenism.* Philadelphia: Fortress, 1974.

P. Vielhauer. *Geschichte der urchristlichen Literatur: Einleitung in das Neue Testament, die Apokrypha und den Apostolischen Vätern.* GL. New York: de Gruyter, 1975.

E. Lohse. *Die Entstehung des Neuen Testaments.* 5th ed. ThW 4. Stuttgart: Kohlhammer, 1991.

J. J. Collins. *The Apocalyptic Imagination: An Introduction to Jewish Apocalyptic Literature.* 2d ed. Grand Rapids: Eerdmans, 1998.

Individual Themes:
H. Bietenhard. *Die himmlische Welt im Urchristentum und Spätjudentum.* WUNT 2. Tübingen: Mohr, 1951.

H. Gese. "Anfang und Ende der Apokalyptik, dargestellt am Sacharjabuch," *ZTK* 70 (1973): 20–49 = Pages 202–30 in *Vom Sinai zum Zion:*

Alttestamentliche Beiträge zur biblischen Theologie. Edited by H. Gese. 3d ed. BEvTh 64. Munich: Kaiser, 1989.

W. Harnisch. *Verhängnis und Verheißung der Geschichte: Untersuchungen zum Zeit- und Geschichtsverständnis im 4. Buch Esra und in der syr. Baruchapokalypse.* FRLANT 97. Göttingen: Vandenhoeck & Ruprecht, 1969.

———. "Der Prophet als Widerpart und Zeuge der Offenbarung: Erwägungen zur Interdependenz von Form und Sache im IV Buch Esra." Pages 461–93 in *Apocalypticism in the Mediterranean World and the Near East: Proceedings of the International Colloquium on Apocalypticism, Uppsala, August 12–17, 1979.* Edited by D. Hellholm. 2d ed. Tübingen: Mohr/Siebeck, 1989.

G. W. E. Nickelsburg. *Resurrection, Immortality, and Eternal Life in Intertestamental Judaism.* HTS 26. Cambridge: Harvard University Press, 1971.

———. "Social Aspects of Palestinian Jewish Apocalypticism." Pages 641–54 in *Apocalypticism in the Mediterranean World and the Near East: Proceedings of the International Colloquium on Apocalypticism, Uppsala, August 12–17, 1979.* Edited by D. Hellholm. 2d ed. Tübingen: Mohr/Siebeck, 1989.

H. C. C. Cavallin. *Life after Death: Paul's Argument for the Resurrection of the Dead in I Cor 15. Part I: An Enquiry into the Jewish Background.* ConBNT 7.1. Lund: Gleerup, 1974.

F. Dexinger. *Henochs Zehnwochenapokalypse und offene Probleme der Apokalyptikforschung.* StPB 29. Leiden: Brill, 1977.

U. Fischer. *Eschatologie und Jenseitserwartungen im Hellenistischen Diasporajudentum.* BZNW 44. New York: de Gruyter, 1978.

P. D. Hanson. *The Dawn of Apocalyptic: The Historical and Sociological Roots of Jewish Apocalyptic Eschatology.* 2d ed. Philadelphia: Fortress, 1979.

M. P. Horgan. *Pesharim: Qumran Interpretations of Biblical Books.* CBQMS 8. Washington: Catholic Biblical Association of America, 1979.

E. Brandenburger. *Die Verborgenheit Gottes im Weltgeschehen: Das literarische und theologische Problem des 4. Esrabuches.* ATANT 68. Zurich: Theologische Verlag Zürich, 1981.

E. Turdeanu. *Apocryphes slaves et roumaines de l'Ancien Testament.* SVTP 5. Leiden: Brill, 1981.

J. Coppens. *Le relève apocalyptique du messianisme royal II: Le fils d'homme vétéro- et intertestamentaire.* BETL 61. Leuven: University Press, 1983.

A. Lacocque. *Daniel et son temps: Recherches sur le mouvement apocalyptique juif au IIe siècle avant Jésus Christ.* MdB. Geneva: Labor et Fides, 1983.

J. J. Collins. *Daniel: With an Introduction to Apocalyptic.* FOTL 20. Grand Rapids: Eerdmans, 1984.

————. *Apocalypticism in the Dead Sea Scrolls.* New York: Routledge, 1997.

J. C. Vanderkam. "Studies in the Apocalypse of Weeks (1 Enoch 93,1–10; 91,11–17)." *CBQ* 46 (1984): 511–23.

M.-Th. Wacker. *Weltordnung und Gericht: Studien zu 1 Henoch 22.* 2d ed. FB 45. Würzburg: Echter, 1985.

K. Müller. *Studien zur frühchristlichen Apokalyptik.* SBAB 11. Stuttgart: Verlag Katholisches Bibelwerk, 1991.

M. Mach. *Entwicklungsstadien des jüdischen Engelglaubens in vorrabbinischer Zeit.* TSAJ 34. Tübingen: Mohr/Siebeck, 1993.

F. García Martínez. *Qumran and Apocalyptic: Studies on the Aramaic Texts from Qumran.* STDJ 9. Leiden: Brill, 1993.

F. García Martínez and J. Trebolle Barrera. *The People of the Dead Sea Scrolls: Their Writings, Beliefs and Practices.* Translated by W. G. E. Watson. Leiden: Brill, 1995.

M. Albani. *Astronomie und Schöpfungsglaube: Untersuchungen zum astronomischen Henochbuch.* WMANT 68. Neukirchen-Vluyn: Neukirchener Verlag, 1996.

M. Albani, J. Frey, and A. Lange, eds. *Studies in the Book of Jubilees.* TSAJ 65. Tübingen: Mohr/Siebeck, 1997.

D. H. Harlow. *The Greek Apocalypse of Baruch (3 Baruch) in Hellenistic Judaism and Early Christianity.* SVTP 12. Leiden: Brill, 1996.

H. Stegemann. *The Library of Qumran: On the Essenes, Qumran, John the Baptist, and Jesus.* (Grand Rapids: Eerdmans, 1998).

5

Deuterocanonical and Postbiblical Psalms

Late- and PostBiblical Psalmody

Thesis: Israel's psalmody was not exhausted by the texts transmitted in the Hebrew Bible but had continued vitality into the later Second Temple period. Only a portion of its witnesses, such as the apocryphal additions to the books of Esther and Daniel, the *Psalms of Solomon,* and the so-called *Five Apocryphal Syriac Psalms,* are transmitted in the Septuagint or the Peshitta. In addition to these, a surprising number of postbiblical psalms have become known through the text discoveries at Qumran.[1]

The *Five Apocryphal Syriac Psalms* (Pss 151–155) and the Prayer of Manasseh

Thesis 1: The Five Apocryphal Syriac Psalms *(Pss 151–155).* The apocryphal Ps 151 transmitted in the Septuagint has a counterpart in the so-called *Syriac Psalms,* which also contain an additional four psalms (Pss 152–155). In addition to Ps 151, the major psalm manuscript 11QPs^a also transmits Pss 154 and 155 in Hebrew. Thus the long-standing suspicion that Pss 151–155 were originally composed in Hebrew has been confirmed. Psalms 151–153 contain dramatic poetry placed in the mouth of David. Psalm 154 is a song of thanksgiving for deliverance from foreigners, and Ps 155 is the lament of a sick individual, secondarily attributed to

---

[1] See the editions by M. Mansoor, *The Thanksgiving Hymns* (STDJ 3; Leiden: Brill, 1961); C. Newsom, *Songs of The Sabbath Sacrifice: A Critical Edition* (HSS 27; Atlanta: Scholars Press, 1985); E. M. Schuller, *Non-canonical Psalms from Qumran: A Pseudepigraphic Collection* (HSS 28; Atlanta: Scholars Press, 1986); and J. A. Sanders, J. H. Charlesworth, and H. W. L. Rietz, "Non-Masoretic Psalms," in *The Dead Sea Scrolls—Hebrew, Aramaic, and Greek Texts with English Translations, 4 A: Pseudepigraphic and Non-Masoretic Psalms and Prayers* (ed. J. H. Charlesworth; Louisville: Westminster John Knox, 1997), 155–85; as well as the translations by F. García Martínez, *The Dead Sea Scrolls Translated* (Leiden: Brill, 1994), 303–78 and 405–30.

Hezekiah. At least Ps 151 is older than the Septuagint translation of the Psalter of the second century B.C.E. Psalm 154 could be of Essene origin or revision, while Ps 155, an exemplary song of individual thanksgiving, could stem either from the Persian or the Hellenistic period.[2]

Issue 1: The Five Apocryphal Syriac Psalms. They were discovered in 1795 in the *Study Book of Elijah of Anbar* but came to the attention of the scholarly world only through the 1887 publication of the manuscript by Wright. As early as 1930, Martin Noth had already contended that all of them trace back to a Hebrew exemplar and offered as evidence a retroversion into Hebrew.[3] The accuracy of this assumption has been confirmed by J. A. Sanders's 1965 publication of the psalm scroll 11QPs[a], which transmits the Hebrew texts of Pss 151, 154, and 155. Debate continues today as to whether the version transmitted in 11QPs[a] or the Greek and Syriac versions better reflect the Hebrew original of Ps 151.[4]

Issue 2: The Genre of Pss 151–155. Psalms 151 (Syr I), 152 (Syr IV), and 153 (Syr V) contain dramatic poetry attributed to David. In Ps 151 (11QPs[a]: Pss 151A and 151B), he reports his life as a shepherd and musician, out of which Yahweh had him anointed, and his victory over Goliath (1 Sam 16–17). Psalm 152 is a lament of the shepherd David on the occasion of his fight with a lion and a bear (1 Sam 17:34–37), and Ps 153 (Syr V) is David's song of thanksgiving after his victory over the two beasts. Psalm 154 (Syr I) consists of an additional song of thanksgiving on the occasion of the deliverance of the poor and blameless from foreign oppressors, and Ps 155 (Syr II) consists of an individual lament seeking healing from leprosy. The two psalms are published as Hezekiah's prayer in only one Syriac manuscript from the twelfth century C.E. This attribution is unsupportable, however, based on the content.

---

[2] On Ps 151 see Sanders, "Non-Masoretic Psalms," 163 (although dating the LXX Psalms in the third century B.C.E. is, indeed, too early); on Ps 154, p. 171, and on Ps 155, p. 179.

[3] M. Noth, "Die fünf syrisch überlieferten apokryphen Psalmen," *ZAW* 48 (1930): 1–23.

[4] See A. S. van der Woude, *JSHRZ* 4.1, 31; and H.-J. Fabry, "11QPs[a] und die Kanonizität des Psalters," in *Freude an der Weisung des Herrn: Beiträge zur Theologie der Psalmen: FS H. Groß* (ed. E. Haag and F.-L. Hossfeld; SBB 13; Stuttgart: Verlag Katholisches Bibelwerk, 1986), 46–67, who speaks for the priority of the text form found in the *Psalms Scroll;* M. Haran, "The Two Text Forms of Psalm 151," *JJS* 39 (1988): 171–82, judges them to be an expansion of the Greek version and, accordingly, to be younger. The relationship is even more complicated as understood by H. F. van Rooy ("Die verhouding van die Siriese Psalm 151 tot de Griekse en Hebreeuse weergaves," *Skrif en Kerk* 18 [1997]: 176–97). He argues that the Hebrew psalm circulated in various versions, one reflected in 11QPs[a] and the other in the Greek translation. In contrast, the Syriac text depends on the Greek but has undergone its own development. Comparison has been made much easier now by the publication of the parallel texts in Sanders et al., *Dead Sea Scrolls,* 163–69.

Bibliography

Text editions:
J. A. Sanders, *The Psalm Scroll of Qumrân Cave 11 (11QPsᵃ).* DJD 4. Oxford: Clarendon, 1965.
W. Baars, ed. *Psalmi Apocryphi.* Vetus Testamentum Syriace iuxta simplicem Syrorum versionem IV/VI. Leiden: Brill, 1972.
Schürer/Vermes 3.1:188–92.
J. A. Sanders, J. H. Charlesworth, and H. W. L. Rietz. "Non-Masoretic Psalms." Pages 155–85 in *The Dead Sea Scrolls: Hebrew, Aramaic, and Greek Texts with English Translations. 4 A: Pseudepigraphic and Non-Masoretic Psalms and Prayers.* Edited by J. H. Charlesworth. Louisville: Westminster John Knox, 1997.

Commentaries:
A. S. van der Woude, JSHRZ, 1974; Charlesworth and Sanders, *OTP* 2, 1985.

Thesis 2: The Prayer of Manasseh. The Prayer of Manasseh is an anthological poem placed in the mouth of the Judean king Manasseh, who, according to 2 Chr 33:11–13, was deported to Babylon and subsequently returned to Jerusalem because of his humble prayer to Yahweh. Analogous to the apocryphal David psalms, this psalm is a dramatic poem. The prayer clearly seems to have been composed in Greek. Its oldest Greek witnesses are the *Apostolic Constitutions* from the fourth and Codex Alexandrinus from the fifth century C.E. The latter offers the Odes in the eighth position. Rahlfs included it in his edition of the Odes in the twelfth position. The absolutely earliest textual witness is the Syriac *Didascalia* from the third century, in which it represents the translation of a lost Greek original from the second century C.E. Some scholars argue that the penitential prayer, which belongs to the genre of individual lament, is of Christian origin. Like the prayers inserted in the Greek Daniel and Esther,[5] it probably owes its origin to the tendency to expand the canonical tradition with appropriate prayers.[6] Luther included it in his complete Bible of 1534 among the Apocrypha.

---

[5] Compare the Prayer of Azariah, a collective penitential prayer inserted in Dan 3:(24)26–45 (cf. also Ezra 9:6–15 and Neh 9:6–37), and the Song of the Three Young Men in the fiery furnace, a hymn transmitted in G Dan 3:(46)52–90 in the form of a litany, as well as the petitionary lament of Mordecai and Esther inserted in G after Esth 4:17, to be regarded as dramatic poetry. See H. Bardtke, *JSHRZ*, 1973; and O. Plöger, *JSHRZ* 1.1; or I. Kottsieper, "Zusätze zu Esther; Zusätze zu Daniel," in *Das Buch Baruch, der Brief des Jeremia, Zusätze zu Esther und Daniel* (ed. O. H. Steck, R. Kratz, and I. Kottsieper; ATD 5; Göttingen: Vandenhoeck & Ruprecht, 1998), 160–86 and 221–47.

[6] E. Osswald, *JSHRZ* 4.1, 20.

Bibliography

Editions of the Text:
W. Baars and H. Schneider, eds. *Oratio Manasse.* Vetus Testamentum syriace iuxta simplicem Syrorum versionem IV/VI. Leiden: Brill, 1972.
A. Rahlfs, ed. *Psalmi cum Odis.* 3d ed. Septuaginta: Vetus Testamentum graecum auctoritate Societatis Scientiarum Gottingensis editum X. Göttingen: Vandenhoeck & Ruprecht, 1979. Pages 361–63.

Introductions:
Oesterley. *Introduction,* 294–99.
Eißfeldt. *Introduction,* 588.
Rost. *EinlApo,* 69–70.
Schürer/Vermes 3.2:730–33.

The Issues:
H. J. Fabry. "11QPsᵃ und die Kanonizität des Psalters." Pages 46–67 in *Freude an der Weisung des Herrn: Beiträge zur Theologie der Psalmen: FS H. Groß.* Edited by E. Haag and F.-L. Hossfeld. SBB 13. Stuttgart: Verlag Katholisches Bibelwerk, 1986.
M. Haran. "The Two Text Forms of Psalm 151." *JJS* 39 (1988): 171–82.
H. F. van Rooy. "Die verhouding van die Siriese Psalm 151 tot de Griekse en Hebreeuse weergaves." *Skrif en Kerk* 18 (1997): 176–97.

Commentaries:
V. Ryssel, *APAT,* 1900; H. Ryle, *APOT,* 1912; E. Osswald, *JSHRZ,* 1974; J. H. Charlesworth, *OTP* 2, 1985.

The *Psalms of Solomon*

Thesis: The *Psalms of Solomon* represents a collection of eighteen songs transmitted only in Greek and Syriac despite their presumed Hebrew origin. They include songs of praise, lament, and thanksgiving that belong to extracultic psalmody. Their character as didactic works reveals the identity of the groups standing behind them. Since *Pss. Sol.* 8 and 17 presume the conquest of Jerusalem by Pompey and *Pss. Sol.* 2 his death, the songs may have originated in the period between 63 and 48, or 70 and 40 B.C.E. The current book may have been composed from them in an act of intentional redaction and composition. The songs are influenced partly, as are the second, eighth, and seventeenth, by passionate animosity toward both the

Hasmonean priest-kings and their vanquishers,[7] partly by the unbridge-able opposition between the righteous and the godless (*Pss. Sol.* 3–6), and finally by the struggle with the problem of theodicy (*Pss. Sol.* 12–16). At the beginning (*Pss. Sol.* 2), in the middle (*Pss. Sol.* 7–11), and at the end (*Pss. Sol.* 17–18) stand psalms dealing with the redemption of Jerusalem and Israel. Despite the skepticism repeatedly expressed recently in regard to the attempts initiated by Wellhausen to find the origin of the psalms among the Pharisees, this hypothesis still deserves attention. The basic theme of the collection consists of petition and thanksgiving in view of the innocent suffering of the righteous, understood as a trial in the context of the expectation of the coming day of judgment and the associated ar-rival of the kingdom of God and resurrection of the dead brought about by the Messiah. As representatives of an eschatologically oriented strict observance of the law, they are an important witness to the backgrounds of the Pharisaic piety that Jesus saw himself as confronting.

Issue 1: The Name of the Book. The song collection owes its name to the late- and postbiblical tendency to impute the authority of King Solomon to song and wisdom literature. The contention of 1 Kgs 5:12 that he com-posed 1008 songs offered such attributions ample room. The current identification is limited to the superscription of the book and of individ-ual psalms and has no support whatsoever in the content of the book.

Comment 1: The Superscriptions and Liturgical Comments. The super-scriptions to *Pss. Sol.* 2–18, lacking in the Syriac text, name Solomon as the author, and the insertions of the *diapsalma (Selah)* in *Pss. Sol.* 17:29 and 18:9 also have no counterpart in the Syriac. They are all secondary at-tempts to harmonize the collection with the Psalter.

Comment 2: The Odes of Solomon *and the Odes.* In order to prevent the obvious confusion of the *Psalms of Solomon* with the *Odes of Solomon* and, in turn, the *Odes of Solomon* with the Odes of the early church transmitted in the Septuagint after the Psalter, it is appropriate to establish here that the *Odes of Solomon* contains the forty-two Christian hymns under the in-fluence of Johannine theology from the late second or early third century C.E.[8] They differ from the nine or fourteen early-church Odes of the Greek

---

[7] See also G. Maier, *Mensch und freier Wille: Nach den jüdischen Religionsparteien zwischen Ben Sira und Paulus* (WUNT 12; Tübingen: Mohr/Siebeck, 1971), 283–85.

[8] See Denis, *Introduction,* 65–66; W. Bauer, "Die Oden Salomos," in *Neutestamentliche Apokryphen in deutscher Übersetzung II* (ed. E. Hennecke and W. Schneemelcher; 3d ed.; Tübingen: 1964), 576–625; and, further, M. Lattke, *Die Oden Salomos in ihrer Bedeu-tung für das Neue Testament* (OBO 25/1a, 3–4; Göttingen: Vandenhoeck & Ruprecht,

church that represent a liturgical collection of Old and New Testament psalms not contained in the Psalter[9] and a Trinitarian morning hymn.

Issue 2: Attestation and Original Language of the Book. The existence of the *Psalms of Solomon* was known in the West before 1626 only from the table of contents of the Septuagint Codex Alexandrinus, which we also thank for the transmission of the early-church Odes. In it, *1* and *2 Clement* followed by the *Psalms of Solomon* are listed after the New Testament with the formula *homo biblia* (together with the books). Presumably, they were thus characterized as noncanonical but in use in the church. Since their rediscovery in a copy of the Codex Vindobonensis Theol. 11 from the tenth century C.E., in which they are found between the Wisdom of Solomon and the Wisdom of Jesus ben Sira, they are attested *in toto* by nine Greek and four Syriac manuscripts from the tenth to the sixteenth centuries C.E., some of which contain only individual songs. Rahlfs's reference edition of the Septuagint places them between Sirach and Hosea, while in the Leiden Peshitta they are included between the *Psalmi apocryphi (Syriac Psalms)* and the book of Tobit.

The unusual verbal syntax, explicable only by means of the hypothesis of a slavish rendition of a Semitic original, and further infelicities in the Greek text, apparently resulting from errors in reading, support the hypothesis that the book was originally composed in Hebrew. Evidence that, primarily if not exclusively, a Hebrew *Vorlage* underlies the Syriac version has recently effectively corrected the usual assessment that the Syriac version represents a secondary translation from the Greek.[10]

Issue 3: The Structure of the Book, Its Genres, Its Sitz im Leben, *and Its Origin.* The *Psalms of Solomon* represent late psalmody serving the self-affirmation of the law-abiding pious in the traumas of the time with its alternating triumphs of the Jewish and pagan godless. Thus, it merits the

---

1980–1998); as well as M. Franzmann, *The Odes of Solomon* (NTOA 20; Göttingen: Vandenhoeck & Ruprecht, 1991).

[9] They are as follows: the Song at the Sea, Exod 15:1–19; Moses' Song, Deut 32:1–43; Hannah's prayer, I Sam 2:1–10; the psalm of Habakkuk, Hab 3:2–19; the psalm of Jonah, Jonah 2:3–10; the Prayer of Azariah, G Dan 3:26–45; the Song of the Three Young Men in the fiery furnace, G Dan 3:52–88; Mary's Magnificat, Luke 1:46–55; Zachariah's Benedictus Deus, Luke 1:68–79; as well as the additions in a few manuscripts of the Song of the Vineyard, Isa 5:1–7, along with the Woe, Isa 5:8f.; Hezekiah's prayer, Isa 38:10–20; the Prayer of Manasseh; Simeon's Nunc Dimittis, Luke 2:29–32 and the early-church morning hymn mentioned above.

[10] See J. L. Trafton, *The Syriac Version of the Psalms of Solomon: A Critical Evaluation* (SBLSCS 11; Atlanta: Scholars Press, 1985), 187–88.

designation "extracultic psalmody."[11] In a stormy epoch of history, the community in which these songs originate is to understand the suffering they innocently experience as the correction of the merciful God and to fix their hope on the imminent Day of Judgment and Mercy (15:12 with 14:9 and 18:5). In it, the godless will meet with eternal annihilation while the God-fearers and the righteous will be delivered and, together with the already deceased pious, rise to eternal life (3:11–12; 13:10–11). In accordance with this temporal situation and intention, one may no longer expect in the *Psalms of Solomon* genres precisely like those of biblical psalmody. The songs sometimes display a complicated composition in which they rework varied genre elements. Among them, the judgment doxology[12] is most prominent. Belief in God's unconditional righteousness, preserved in this as well as in the coming life, comprises the core of the eschatological expectations of the community.

The intentional alternation between individual and collective psalms reveals both the artfulness of the book's composition as well as its message.[13] From a formal perspective, the lament of Jerusalem that opens the book in *Pss. Sol.* 1 precedes five individual psalms in 2–6, then five collective psalms in 7–11, and, once again in 12–16, five individual psalms. The collection concludes with two collective psalms, *Pss. Sol.* 17 and 18:1–9. *Psalms of Solomon* 18:10–12 constitutes the presumably secondary hymnic conclusion to the whole collection.

Thus, Zion's lament in *Pss. Sol.* 1 finds its initial response in the individual song of thanksgiving that reports Jerusalem's guilt and punishment and its preservation from total annihilation. *Psalms of Solomon* 3–6 draws life from the contrast between the righteous and the godless, characterized in sequence in 3 and 4. Meanwhile, 3 and 6 are hymns and 4 and 5 are songs of individual lament. In contrast, the second block of individual psalms in 12–16 revolves around the theme of God's righteousness. In *Pss. Sol.* 12 and 13, songs of individual lament and of individual thanksgiving alternate with one another. A hymn follows in 14. The two songs of individual thanksgiving in *Pss. Sol.* 15 and 16 conclude the second block of individual psalms. The middle block with five collective psalms in 7–11 opens with the two songs of collective lament, *Pss. Sol.* 7 and 8, both of

---

[11] See F. Stolz, *Psalmen im nachkultischen Raum* (ThSt 129; Zürich: Theologische Verlag Zürich, 1983), 27–29. One must understand the term "postcultic" in this case to permit the use of the songs in community gatherings of the pious but to exclude it in the performance of the ritual temple cult.

[12] See 2:15–21; 8:25–34; 10:5–8.

[13] See also P. N. Franklyn, "The Cultic and Pious Climax of Eschatology in the Psalms of Solomon," *JSJ* 18 (1987): 1–17.

which petition God for mercy for Jerusalem or Israel. At the center of this group stands the collective lament in 9 with the confession of the righteousness of God manifest in Israel's exile and the petition that God have mercy on his chosen people Israel. The hymn *Pss. Sol.* 10 calls the pious to praise God, who has mercy on the poor. The eleventh psalm proleptically proclaims the return of the redeemed to Zion. The nationalist line, continued through the collective lament in *Pss. Sol.* 17 and the hymnic praise of God, whose goodness governs Israel and preserves it in the day of his mercy, concludes in 18:1–9.

Thus the composition already reveals the intention of the collection to strengthen the righteous in the hope of Israel's redemption and the subsequent annihilation of the godless and, simultaneously, in their own fidelity to the law, especially since God's righteousness has already now been displayed in the end of the foreign conqueror and of the usurped reign of their own rulers. Only this intention explains why the second song, which contains the latest contemporary allusion, follows directly on Jerusalem's initial lament. Furthermore, the alternation between the individual and the collective psalms indicates that the book is intended to serve both the devotion of individuals and the instruction and comfort of the community to which the songs owe their eschatologically oriented law-piety. The differences in the genre and time in *Pss. Sol.* 8 versus 17 and 2 and the well-planned construction of the collection reveal that they owe their current form to a redactional process.[14]

Issue 4. Dating the Psalms of Solomon. The contemporaneous allusions in *Pss. Sol.* 2, 8, and 17 permit the determination of the time of origin for the song collection. According to *Pss. Sol.* 17:55, the Davidic monarchy had been usurped by unqualified men. A foreigner described as lawless had deported the usurpers along with their children to the West. The homeland of the conqueror, against whom the rulers of the land marched according to 8:15–22 and whom they had festively received in Jerusalem, lay in the West as well. According to 2:1–2, the temple was besieged and conquered by the sinful foreigner and defiled by his soldiers. According to 2:26–31, the conqueror himself was later murdered on the Egyptian coast. All these allusions can only refer to the occupation of Jerusalem by Pompey in 63 B.C.E. and his death in 48 B.C.E. On his campaign against Jerusalem, in

---

14 J. Schüpphaus (*Die Psalmen Salomo: Ein Zeugnis jerusalemer Theologie und Frömmigkeit in der Mitte des vorchristlichen Jahrhunderts* [ALGHJ 7. Leiden: Brill, 1977], 138–58) has attempted to explain the tensions within and among the songs as the result of a redactional revision and expansion of a collection initially comprising *Pss. Sol.* 1–2; 8; 17 and 4; 5:5–7; 7; 9; 11 and 12.

whose temple the adherents of Aristobulus II had entrenched themselves, Aristobulus's brother Hyrcanus II welcomed him ceremoniously into the city. Subsequently, Pompey conquered the temple and entered it. He held Aristobulus II in custody in order to deport him along with his family and adherents to Rome. Finally, during his flight from Caesar in 48 B.C.E., Pompey was murdered while disembarking his ship at the Egyptian coast. In contrast to the hyperbolic assumption made in *Pss. Sol.* 2:27, however, one of his officers arranged his funeral pyre (Plutarch, *Pomp.* 78–80). The animosity of the community standing behind the songs toward the Hasmonean ruling house can be explained, at any rate, as a response to what the pious felt was its usurpation of both the high priesthood and the monarchy (8:11 and 17:5–6). Presumably the removal of favor from the Pharisees under John Hyrcanus, their persecution by Alexander Jannaeus, and the partisan alignment of his son Aristobulus II with the Sadducees also played roles. Since an undelivered speech in praise of Alexander Jannaeus has been found in Cave 4 at Qumran (4Q448),[15] the pious who, according to 17:16, fled the throne usurper can hardly have been Essenes but must have been Pharisees. Furthermore, one can identify the law-abiding community characterized by imminent eschatological expectations mirrored in the *Psalms of Solomon* with the Pharisees with a great deal of probability. The fact that the *Psalms of Solomon* are not represented in the discoveries at Qumran supports this, as does the fact that the expectation of a high-priestly messiah alongside the Davidic messiah in the end time, typical of the Qumran Essenes, is absent in them.[16]

---

[15] See Stegemann, *Library of Qumran*, 159–60; text in translation in J. Maier, *Die Qumran Essener: Texte vom Toten Meer III* (UTB 1863; Munich: Reinhardt, 1995), 526.

[16] Regarding the discussion initiated by J. Wellhausen, *The Pharisees and the Sadducees: An Examination of Internal Jewish History* (Macon, Ga.: Mercer University Press, 2001), 99–106; concerning authorship, see R. Deines, *Die Pharisäer: Ihr Verständnis im Spiegel der christlichen und jüdischen Forschung seit Wellhausen und Graetz* (WUNT 101; Tübingen: Mohr/Siebeck, 1993). The attempt by W. Frankenberg (*Die Datierung der Psalmen Salomos: Ein Beitrag zur jüdischen Geschichte* [BZAW 1; Gießen: Richer, 1896], 9–12) to relate the allusions to the time of Antiochus IV already fails since, in context, *Pss. Sol.* 2:26–35 can only be understood as a fulfillment report but not, like Dan 11:45, as a prediction and Antiochus cannot be identified with an enemy from the West in accordance with 17:12. In the meantime, A. Caquot ("Les Hasmonéens, les Romains et Hérode: Observations sur Ps.Sal.17," in *Hellenica et Judaica: Hommâge à V. Nikiprowetzky* [ed. A. Caquot, M. Hadas-Lebel, and J. Riaud; Paris: Editions Peters, 1986], 213–18), and K. Atkinson ("Herod the Great, Sosius and the Siege of Jerusalem (37 B.C.) in Psalm of Solomon 17," *NTS* 44 [1998]: 557–77, as well as K. Atkinson, "On the Herodian Origin of Militant Davidic Messianism at Qumran: New Light from *Psalm of Solomon* 17," *JBL* 118 [1999]: 435–60) have argued that *Pss. Sol.* 17:4–20 refers to Herod the Great's conquest of Jerusalem in 37 B.C.E. (Atkinson) or to the consequences of the famine during his reign (25 B.C.E.), respectively.

Issue 5: The Theology of the Psalms of Solomon. The concerns of the *Psalms of Solomon* have already been outlined in Issue 3. For these songs, God is primarily the unconditionally righteous judge who requites every person according to his or her deeds and thus punishes the godless already now as well as on the Day of Judgment (2:8, 18; 8:7–8; 9:5, 10; and 17:8). At the same time, however, God is merciful and gracious to his devotees (2:33–37; 4:25; 5:2, 15; and 18:1). Since God nourishes the whole world (5:9–19), he is especially the hope of the poor and needy (5:11; 18:2). Whoever asks him to avenge the deeds of the enemy can already experience his righteous judgment now (compare 2:22–25 with 2:26–34; 9:5–11; further 4:6–8). Indeed, God also corrects the righteous who must recognize that their suffering represents the visitation of their own sins hidden even from themselves (3:4–8; 7:3–10; and 10:5). Meanwhile, in every case, the promise of eternal life can comfort whoever keeps God's commandments (14:1–5); on the coming Judgment Day, all sinners will perish (3:11; 15:12) while God will demonstrate his mercy to the righteous (14:9–10), give them eternal life (13:10), and resurrect the righteous dead (3:12).

According to 17:21–25 judgment on the unrighteous princes and pagan intruders in Jerusalem will be performed by the king, a son of David raised up by God. The king will then rule in absolute righteousness over his people and the peoples of the world solely by the power of his word. All the nations will serve him and bring him the Jews of the Diaspora as their gifts. This king will draw his strength, however, from the fact that he allows the Lord to be his king (17:34).[17] Thus here the Davidic kingdom of the end times is incorporated into and subordinated to the kingdom of God. It therefore fulfills the royal ideal of Isa 9:1–6 and 11:1–5 as well as that of the Chronicler, for whom the earthly king was a placeholder for the kingdom of God (1 Chr 17:14). The *Psalms of Solomon* is admittedly not an eschatological pamphlet, but a book of comfort and a school of prayer for the pious battered by the chaos of their time.

---

[17] See E.-J. Waschke, "'Richte ihnen auf ihren König, den Sohn Davids'—Psalmen Salomos 17 und die Frage nach den messianischen Traditionen," in *Reformation und Neuzeit: 300 Jahre Theologie in Halle* (ed. U. Schnelle; New York: de Gruyter, 1994), 31–46.

Bibliography

Editions of the Text:

Greek:

O. von Gebhardt. *Die Psalmen Salomos.* Augsburg 1871 (incorporated in A. Rahlfs, *Septuaginta: Id est, Vetus Testamentum graece iuxta LXX intrepretes, II* [Stuttgart: Deutsche Bibelgesellschaft, 1935] 471–89).

Syriac:

W. Baars. "The Psalms of Solomon," in *The Old Testament in Syriac according to the Peshitta Version.* IV/6. Leiden: Brill, 1972.

Introduction:

Steuernagel. *Lehrbuch der Einleitung in das Alte Testament mit einem Anhang über den Apokryphen un Pseudepigraphen.* Tübingen: Mohr, 1912. Pages 805–7.

Eißfeldt. *Introduction,* 610–13.

A.-M. Denis. *Introduction aux pseudépigraphes grecs d'Ancien Testament.* SVTP 1. Leiden: Brill, 1970. Pages 60–64.

Rost. *EinlApo,* 89–91.

Schürer/Vermes. 3.1:192–97.

The Issues:

W. Frankenberg. *Die Datierung der Psalmen Salomos: Ein Beitrag zur jüdischen Geschichte.* BZAW 1. Gießen: Ricker, 1896.

K. G. Kuhn. *Die älteste Textgestalt der Psalmen Salomos, insbesondere aufgrund der syrischen Übersetzung neu untersucht, mit einer Bearbeitung und Übersetzung der PsSal.13–17.* BWANT 21. Stuttgart: Kohlhammer, 1937.

H. L. Jansen. *Die spätjüdische Psalmendichtung, ihr Entstehungskreis und ihr 'Sitz im Leben': Eine literargeschichtlich-soziologische Untersuchung.* SNVAO 1937/3. Oslo: Dybwad, 1937.

J. Begrich. "Der Text der Psalmen Salomos." *ZNW* 38 (1939): 131–64.

H. Braun. "Vom Erbarmen Gottes über den Gerechten: Zur Theologie der Psalmen Salomos." *ZNW* 43 (1950/1951): 1–54.

J. O'Dell. "The Religious Background of the Psalms of Solomon: Reevaluated in the Light of the Qumran Texts." *RevQ* 9 (1961): 241–57.

S. Holm-Nielsen. "Erwägungen zu dem Verhältnis zwischen den Hodajot und den Psalmen Salomos." Pages 112–31 in *Bibel und Qumran:*

Beiträge zur Erforschung der Beziehungen zwischen Bibel und Qumran-wissenschaft: Hans Bardtke zum 22.9.1966. Edited by S. Wagner. Berlin: Evangelische Haupt-Bibelgesellschaft, 1965.

J. Wellhausen. *Die Pharisäer und die Sadduzäer: Eine Untersuchung zur inneren jüdischen Geschichte.* 3d ed. Göttingen: Vandenhoeck & Ruprecht, 1967.

G. Maier, *Mensch und freier Wille: Nach den jüdischen Religionsparteien zwischen Ben Sira und Paulus.* WUNT 12. Tübingen: Mohr/Siebeck, 1971.

R. B. Wright. "The Psalms of Solomon, the Pharisees, and the Essenes." Pages 136–54 in *1972 Proceedings of the International Organization for Septuagint and Cognate Studies.* Edited by Robert Kraft. Philadelphia: SBL, 1972.

J. Schüpphaus. *Die Psalmen Salomo: Ein Zeugnis jerusalemer Theologie und Frömmigkeit in der Mitte des vorchristlichen Jahrhunderts.* ALGHJ 7. Leiden: Brill, 1977.

R. R. Hann. *The Manuscript History of the Psalms of Solomon.* SBLSCS 13. Chico: Scholars Press, 1982.

———. "The Community of the Pious: The Social Setting of the Psalms of Solomon." *SR* 17 (1988): 169–89.

F. Stolz. *Psalmen im nachkultischen Raum.* ThSt 129. Zürich: Theologische Verlag Zürich, 1983.

J. L. Trafton. *The Syriac Version of the Psalms of Solomon: A Critical Evaluation.* SBLSCS 11. Atlanta: Scholars Press, 1985.

A. Caquot. "Les Hasmonéens, les Romains et Hérode: Observations sur Ps.Sal.17." Pages 213–18 in *Hellenica et Judaica: Hommage à V. Nikiprowetzky.* Edited by A. Caquot, M. Hadas-Lebel, and J. Riaud. Paris: Éditions Peters, 1986.

P. N. Franklyn. "The Cultic and Pious Climax of Eschatology in the Psalms of Solomon." *JSJ* 18 (1987): 1–17.

M. de Jonge. "The Expectation of the Future in the Psalms of Solomon." *Neot* 21 (1989): 93–117.

E.-J. Waschke. "'Richte ihnen auf ihren König, den Sohn Davids'— Psalmen Salomos 17 und die Frage nach den messianischen Traditionen." Pages 31–46 in *Reformation und Neuzeit: 300 Jahre Theologie in Halle.* Edited by U. Schnelle. New York: de Gruyter, 1994.

R. Deines. *Die Pharisäer: Ihr Verständnis im Spiegel der christlichen und jüdischen Forschung seit Wellhausen und Graetz.* WUNT 101. Tübingen: Mohr/Siebeck, 1997.

K. Atkinson. "Herod the Great, Sosius and the Siege of Jerusalem (37 B.C.) in Psalm of Solomon 17." *NTS* 44 (1998): 313–22.

————. "On the Herodian Origin of Militant Davidic Messianism at Qumran: New Light from *Psalm of Solomon* 17." *JBL* 118 (1999): 435–60.

Commentaries:
R. Kittel, *APAT,* 1900; G. B. Gray, *APOT,* 1913; W. Bauer, *NTApo,* 1964³; S. Holm-Nielsen, *JSHRZ,* 1977; R. B. Wright, *OTP.* 1985; P. Prigent, "Psaumes de Salomon." Pages 943–92 in *La Bible: Écrits Intertestamentaires.* Edited by A. Dupont-Sommer et al. Paris: Gallimard, 1987.

6

Deuterocanonical Wisdom Books

Sirach (Ecclesiasticus)

Thesis 1: The Book of Jesus Ben Sira. The book designated in the Greek and Syriac manuscripts as the *Wisdom of Jesus Son of Sira,* or as the *Wisdom of Ben Sira* and in the Vulgate as *Liber Jesu filii Sirach* or *Ecclesiasticus* was not included in the Hebrew canon and was excluded from use in synagogue worship because of its unequivocally late origins. Consequently, Protestants assign it to the Apocrypha and Catholics to the deuterocanonical writings.

Thesis 2: Character and Significance of the Book. The book, composed by a scribe and wisdom teacher, is an important witness to the intellectual and social situation of Jerusalemite Judaism in the first quarter of the second century B.C.E. Although oriented in form[1] and content toward biblical models,[2] it contains a whole series of new, time-specific themes. As indicated not for the last time by the Praise of the Fathers in Sir 44:1–50:24, despite its avoidance of an explicit dialogue with Greco-Hellenistic thought, the book pursues the intention of preserving among the aristocratic youth of his people, but not among them alone, self-confidence in their Jewish identity against the challenges of Hellenism. With its realistic assessment of the behavior of the rich and powerful toward the poor, its teaching suggests that the author did not turn solely to members of the upper class, to

---

[1] Regarding the literary forms, such as the didactic discourses composed of individual sayings, autobiographical and didactic narratives, as well as onomastic lists, and the hymns and petitionary prayers, see P. W. Skehan and A. A. Di Lella, AB 39, 21–30; further W. Baumgartner, "Die literarischen Gattungen in der Weisheit des Jesus Sirach," *ZAW* 34 (1914): 161–98; and E. G. Bauckmann, "Die Proverbien und die Sprüche des Jesus Sirach," *ZAW* 72 (1960): 33–63.

[2] On its biblical allusions, see T. Middendorp, *Die Stellung Jesu Ben Siras zwischen Judentum und Hellenismus* (Leiden: Brill, 1973), 35–91. Regarding the question of whether Ben Sira knew Qoheleth, see, recently, J. Marböck, "Kohelet und Sirach," in *Das Buch Kohelet* (ed. L. Schwienhorst-Schönberger; BZAW 254; New York: de Gruyter, 1997), 275–331, esp. 275–81.

which, as a scribe, he may have also belonged.[3] Definitive of his theology is the conviction that all the wisdom of the world comes from the Lord, that the Torah is its source, and that the way to it is the fear of the Lord expressed in keeping the commandments. Against this background, the wise man unfolds his concrete instructions for a proper, successful, and divinely blessed life.

Issue 1: The Text and Textual Transmission of Book.[4] The complete text of the book is extant in the major Septuagint manuscripts of the fourth and fifth centuries C.E. It traces back to the Greek translation of the Hebrew original prepared by the grandson of the wise man. It dates to sometime after 138 at the earliest, but probably to sometime after 117 B.C.E. The manuscript fragments from the caves at Qumran and from Masada represent the oldest Hebrew witnesses to the text. Additionally, manuscript fragments from the genizah of the Karaite synagogue in old Cairo attest to at least two text forms.[5] Thus 68 percent of the text survives in Hebrew. The Old Latin (Vetus Latina) text finally included in the Vulgate attests an expanded Greek, and the Syriac reflects an edited Hebrew form of the text. Since even the oldest Greek form of the text is free of neither misunderstandings nor inconsistencies in translation and textual corruptions, the determination of the text essentially requires a circumspect comparison of the entire textual tradition.

Comment 1: The Textual Transmission of the Book of Sirach. From the prologue prefaced to his translation by the grandson of Ben Sira, it has long been known that the book was composed in Hebrew. Jerome still had access to the Hebrew text. Yet apart from rabbinic citations, it remained unknown until Schechter's 1896 discovery in the genizah of the Ezra Synagogue in old Cairo of manuscript fragments stemming from the eleventh

---

[3] See V. Tcherikover, *Hellenistic Civilization and the Jews* (trans. S. Applebaum; Philadelphia: JPS, 1959; repr. Peabody, Mass.: Hendrickson, 1999), 142–51; J. J. Collins, *Jewish Wisdom in the Hellenistic Age* (Louisville: Westminster John Knox, 1997), 29–32; as well as A. Minissale, "Ben Siras Selbstverständnis in Bezug auf Autoritäten der Gesellschaft," in *Der Einzelne und seine Gemeinschaft bei Ben Sira* (ed. R. Egger-Wenzel and R. Krammer; BZAW 270; New York: de Gruyter, 1998), 103–15; regarding its concepts of poverty and wealth, see also V. M. Asensio, "Poverty and Wealth: Ben Sira's View of Possessions," in *Der Einzelne,* 151–78.

[4] See the overview in Skehan and Di Lella, AB 39, 51–62; or, concisely, G. Sauer, JSHRZ 3.5, 484–87. On the state of the discussion, see F. V. Reiterer, "Review of Recent Research on the Book of Ben Sira (1980–1996)," in *The Book of Ben Sira in Modern Research: Proceedings of the First International Ben Sira Conference, 28–31 July 1996, Soesterberg, Netherlands* (ed. P. C. Beentjes; BZAW 255; New York: de Gruyter, 1997), 26–34.

[5] See St. C. Reif, "The Discovery of the Cambridge Genizah Fragments of Ben Sira: Scholars and Texts," in *Research* (ed. Beentjes), 1–22.

and twelfth centuries C.E. Fragments of six manuscripts (H^A-F^) have since been published. Meanwhile, thanks to this discovery, 68 percent of the Hebrew text is now available. Investigations of the fragments have shown that some of them (such as the Qumran and Masada fragments and the marginal readings of H^B^)[6] mirror the original Hebrew text (H I) and some contain later expansions and reinterpretations (H II).

The major Septuagint manuscripts from the fourth to the fifth centuries C.E. still offer the oldest complete form of the text. The sequence of the text is disturbed in all Greek manuscripts, however, by the erroneous insertion, which occurred in the root manuscript, of the pages containing 33:13b–36:13a between 30:26 and 30:27. The entire Greek textual tradition mirrors a discrepancy analogous to that in the medieval Hebrew texts. Essentially the more concise version (G I) in the major manuscripts is the older. They may trace primarily to the grandson of Ben Sira and thus to H I. Yet even this form of the text is not free from misunderstandings and secondary reinterpretations. The expanded and later form of the text (G II), whose additions are not offered in entirety by any single Greek manuscript, apparently already assumes H II but also attests H I. As long as the Hebrew text of the book is only available in fragments, the text of the Septuagint comprises the starting point for any academic study of the book of Sirach.

The Syriac text of the Peshitta is based on a Hebrew exemplar. Although it already knew the expanded text of H II and displays additions characteristic of it, it has significance in isolated cases for the reconstruction of H I. Michael M. Winter has shown that post-Nicene influences underlie the Syriac's revision of statements concerning the creation of wisdom.[7] In contrast, his attempt to attribute the primary Syriac translation to the Ebionites raises objections.[8] Since the Arabic daughter translation of the Peshitta seems to have remained free of secondary alterations under the influence of G II, it is, in the judgment of Hans-Peter Rüger, an important aid in the reconstruction of the original Syriac text.[9]

The Old Latin is a problematic witness to the text. It appears to be based on the G I text and does not yet contain the later exchange of the

---

[6] See C. Martone, "The Ben Sira Manuscripts from Qumran and Masada," in *Research* (ed. Beentjes), 81–94.

[7] See M. M. Winter, "The Origins of Ben Sira in Syriac (Part I)," *VT* 27 (1977): 237–53; M. M. Winter, "The Origins of Ben Sira in Syriac (Part II)," *VT* 27 (1977): 494–507.

[8] Compare Winter, "Origins (Part I)," 237–53, with R. J. Owens, "The Early Syriac Text of Ben Sira in the Demonstrations of Aphrahat," *JSS* 34 (1989): 39–75.

[9] Compare H.-P. Rüger. *Text und Textform im hebräischen Sirach: Eine Untersuchung zur Textgeschichte und Textkritik der hebräischen Sirachfragmente aus der Kairoer Geniza* (BZAW 112; New York: de Gruyter, 1970), 107.

pages containing 30:27–33 with those containing 33:13b–36:16a. Otherwise, however, it has fallen under the influence of G II. The original version of the Old Latin contains neither the prologue nor the Praise of the Fathers. Since Jerome did not produce a new translation, the Old Latin text, supplemented with the prologue and chapters 44–50, was included in the Vulgate.

In view of this transmission history, the original text of the book of Sirach is not simply a given for the exegete but must be deduced in many cases by means of a careful examination of the textual witnesses.

Comment 2: Citations of the Book. The reader of the Septuagint must remember that in the hypothetical original manuscript the pages containing Sir 33:13b–36:13a were erroneously inserted between 30:26 and 30:27. Conversely, versification of the genizah fragments does not always agree with the Septuagint. In order to diminish, or at least not to intensify, the resulting confusion, citations should essentially follow the edition of the Göttingen Septuagint prepared by Joseph Ziegler. In the area of 33:13b–36:13a his versification, following the Vulgate and placed in square brackets, should be employed.[10]

Issue 2: Name and Placement of the Book. In Greek and Syriac manuscripts, the book is designated the *Wisdom of Jesus the Son of Sirach* or the *Wisdom of the Son of Sirach.* According to Jerome, the Hebrew manuscript available to him bore the title *Parabolae,* that is, *Meshalim* or *Sayings.* Yet the second colophon in H^B 51:30c-e confirms the classical title. The Septuagint situates the book between the Wisdom of Solomon and the *Psalms of Solomon.*

Comment 3: The Name of the Author. The name of the author is transmitted variously. In the two colophons of manuscript H^B in 50:27a and 51:30c-e, he is called Simon ben Jeshua ben Eleazer ben Sira'. In contrast, the only G colophon in 50:27c calls him Jesus, son of Sirach Eleazer, the Jerusalemite. In 51:30c-e, the Syriac calls the author Jeshua, son of Simon, the Bar Ezira, and then repeats the title of the book as *Wisdom of Bar Sira'.* In view of the tradition's uncertainty, one must follow the grandson who, in Prologue 7, calls his grandfather Jesus. Presumably, the tradition of the name in H II influenced S and finally also G. Conversely, the tradition of G I/H I secondarily influenced H II and S. In the event that one does not

---

[10] See the synopsis of versification by F. V. Reiterer, *Zähl-synopse zum Buch Ben Sira* (New York: de Gruyter, 2003).

consider the proper names and the expanded genealogy of H II to be merely the result of confusion, one can assume at any rate that Sirach was not the father but the grandfather or ancestor of the author. In view of the divergence in the tradition, therefore, it is often preferred to designate him as Ben Sira.[11]

Issue 3: The Person and Time of Ben Sira. As can be inferred from the grandson's Prologue 8–10, from the praise of the wise *sofer* in Sir 38:24–39:11, and from the apparent familiarity of the author with the biblical tradition,[12] Jesus Sirach was a writer or scribe. Whether he was of priestly origin is disputed. His literary activity apparently fell in the period between 195 and 185 B.C.E.

Comment 4: The Person of Ben Sira. The grandson reports in Prologue 7–12 that his grandfather was a man who had acquired "knowledge of the Law and the Prophets and the other books of the fathers," and who could consequently write about education and wisdom. This characterization finds confirmation and concretization in the praise of the *sofer,* the scribe, in Sir 38:24–39:12. According to this passage, Ben Sira himself apparently belonged among the scribes who not only taught what was right on the basis of their knowledge of the Torah but also rendered judgment in court and, thanks to their knowledge of the practices of foreign peoples and lands and to their life experience, were the professional teachers of their contemporaries, adults as well as youth (compare Sir 36:16a–30:27 with, for example, 6:18). Although, judging from Sir 7:29–31, 32(35):1–26, 45:6–24, and 50:1–21, Ben Sira greatly respected the priestly office and the sacrificial cult and assigned instruction in the Torah and judicial responsibilities to the scribe as well as to the priest (compare Sir 38:33; 39:8 with 45:17 and 26), it is not certain that he was a priestly scribe. The cultic aspect recedes in 38:24–39:11 behind that of personal piety and wisdom. Besides, the book contains no direct exegesis of the Torah.[13] To the extent that one may consider the autobiographically styled poem in 51:13–20 as Ben Sira's

---

[11] See the extensive treatment by F. V. Reiterer, *Bibliographie zu Ben Sira* (BZAW 266; New York: de Gruyter, 1998), 1–10.

[12] See n. 2 above.

[13] See H. Stadelmann, *Ben Sira als Schriftgelehrter: Eine Untersuchung zum Berufsbild des vor-makkabäischen Sofer unter Berücksichtigung seines Verhältnisses zu Priester-, Propheten- und Weisheitslehrtum* (WUNT 2/6; Tübingen: Mohr/Siebeck, 1980), 271–93, who calls attention expressly in this sense to apologetic interests in defending the reputation of the scribe and the priest; but see the refutations by J. Marböck, *Gottes Weisheit unter uns: Zur Theologie des Buches Sirach* (HBS 6; New York: Herder, 1995), 38–39; and Collins, *Jewish Wisdom,* 37. O. Wischmeyer (*Kultur des Buches Jesus Sirach* [BZNW 77; New York: de Gruyter, 1995], 47 n. 55), does not exclude the possibility that Ben Sirach was a physician.

personal testimony and not understand the expression metaphorically, he could have been active in a house of instruction *(bêt hammidrash)*. On the other hand, it is worthy of consideration whether he should be understood, on the model of Hellenistic philosophers, as a tutor of youthful adherents.[14] His realistic evaluation of the misuse of power and wealth may suggest, according to Victor Tcherikover and John J. Collins, that he did not belong to the upper class but owed his career to his expertise.[15]

Comment 5: The Date of Ben Sira. For dating, the grandson's external witness is determinative. He reports in Prologue 27 that he came to Egypt in the thirty-eighth year of King Euergetes. Now, two Ptolemies adopted the designation Euergetes, "the Beneficent": Ptolemy III (246–221 B.C.E.) and Ptolemy VIII. The latter reigned from 170 to 164 B.C.E., in 145/144 as co-regent with his brother Ptolemy VII Physicon, and then from 145 to 116 B.C.E. as sole ruler. Since Ptolemy III held the throne only twenty-five years, he and, thus the third century, can be ruled out as the period of Ben Sira's activity. Starting with the year 170 as the beginning of the reign of Ptolemy VIII, the grandson of Ben Sira came to Egypt in 132 B.C.E. Now, however, the information that he "was contemporary with him" in Prologue 28 seems to presume that the grandson prepared the translation of the book only after the death of Ptolemy VIII in 116 B.C.E. If one assumes that the grandson was about thirty when he came to Egypt and that the average duration of a generation amounts to approximately thirty years, one arrives at the first quarter of the second century B.C.E. as the time of Ben Sira's activity. This calculation agrees with the information from his book itself. On the one hand, in his eulogy of the high priest Simon son of Johanan/Onias in 50:1–21 concluding the Praise of the Fathers, Ben Sira already presupposes Simon's death. The subject of the eulogy was Simon II, who, according to the testimony of Flavius Josephus *(Ant.* 12.224), held the high-priestly office early in the second century. On the other hand, Ben Sira does not yet know of the removal (175 B.C.E.) of Simon's son and successor, Onias III, and the associated attempts at hellenization by the new high priest Jason,[16] even though his book already reflects Hellenism's influence on Judaism. Therefore, Ben Sira's literary activity may fall in the period between 190 and 180 B.C.E.

---

[14] On Ben Sirach's school, see Collins, *Jewish Wisdom,* 36–39.

[15] Tcherikover, *Hellenistic Civilization and the Jews,* 148; Reiterer, "Review," 36; and Collins, *Jewish Wisdom,* 29–32.

[16] See K. Bringmann, *Hellenistische Reform und Religionsverfolgung: Eine Untersuchung zur jüdisch-hellenistischen Geschichte (175–165 v.Chr.)* (AAWG 3.132; Göttingen: Vandenhoeck & Ruprecht, 1983).

Issue 4: Scope and Structure of the Book. The book of Sirach contains fifty-one chapters. Apart from the prologue prefixed to the Greek translation, it falls into three sections: (1) the didactic speeches of chapters 1–43; (2) the Praise of the Fathers in chapters 44–50 together with the first colophon in 50:27–29; and (3) the prayer of Ben Sira in 51:1–12 and the alphabetic/acrostic song in praise of wisdom in 51:13–30, after which H[B] and the Syriac offer a second colophon.

Comment 6: The Structure of the Book. The first section, chapters 1–43, can be subdivided into chapters 1–23 and 24–43. The Praise of Wisdom in chapter 24 marks the caesura between the two subdivisions. Notably, in chapters 1–43 repeated sections with general content emphasizing the importance of wisdom or the activity of God alternate with those that contain specific life lessons. Besides 1:1–10, 20–33 and 24:1–33, general material occurs in 4:11–19, 6:18–37, 14:20–15:10, 32:14–33:18, 39:12–35, and 42:15–43:33. Of these, 1:1–10, 20–33 and 42:15–43:33 frame the lessons contained in 1:11–42:14, while chapter 24 stands in the middle of the didactic material in the first section. At the same time, 1:1–10 together with the prayer of Ben Sira in 51:1–12 forms the outer framework surrounding the whole book. The wisdom pericopes[17] and hymns between them seem, in contrast, to mark new beginnings. Thus, the entire book can be subdivided as follows:[18]

1.1	1:1–4:10	Wisdom as fear of the Lord[19]
1.2	4:11–6:17	Everyday wisdom[20]
1.3	6:18–14:19	Striving for everyday wisdom
1.4	14:20–23:17	God's wisdom and human wisdom and folly
2.1	24:1–32:13	Wisdom as guide in all life situations
2.2	32:14–39:11	On divine and human concern
2.3	39:12–43:44	God's creation and human joy and sorrow
2.4	44:1–50:24	Praise of the Fathers

---

[17] See O. Rickenbacher, *Weisheitsperikopen bei Ben Sira* (OBO 1; Göttingen: Vandenhoeck & Ruprecht, 1973); and Collins, *Jewish Wisdom,* 46–54.

[18] See also the structural analysis in Wischmeyer, *Kultur,* 151–53. For the current discussion concerning the structure of the book, see Marböck, "Structure and Redaction History," in *Research* (ed. P. C. Beentjes), 61–79; and concisely Reiterer, "Review," 37–39.

[19] See also Marböck, *Gottes Weisheit,* 69–72.

[20] See also Marböck, *Gottes Weisheit,* 72–74.

3.1   50:25–29   First epilogue, the nations saying (vv. 25–26)
                   and first colophon (vv. 27–29)

3.2   51:1–12   Appendix, prayer of Sira. In praise of wisdom
                   (vv. 13–30a). Second colophon (v. 30b–e)

Comment 7: Themes of the Mottoes and Summary Texts. The reader will soon determine that the thematization of the sections is an attempt to understand the concrete life lessons in relation to wisdom theological mottoes. Since a more extensive subdivision and list of the themes treated in the concrete life lessons would go too far here,[21] the following will indicate at least the pertinent mottoes and, in certain cases, also the summaries: 1:1–10, the origin of wisdom; 1:11–30, the fear of God and wisdom; 2:1–18, fear of God and trust in God; 4:11–19, the teaching and admonition of wisdom; 6:18–37, admonition to study wisdom; 14:20–15:10, the search for wisdom and its blessing; 15:11–16:23, human free will and responsibility; 16:24–18:14, God's creative wisdom and gifts to humans; 23:1–6, prayer for wisdom's discipline; 24:1–34, praise of wisdom and its identification with the Torah; 32:14–33:18, on God's election; 36:1–22, prayer for the return of the tribes of Jacob and the glorification of Zion; 39:12–35, praise of the Creator and his providence; 42:15–43:33, praise of God's creative work.

Issue 5: Indications of the Stages in the Book's Growth.[22] The formal and thematic unity of the discourses, theological reflections, and hymns (such as the praise of wisdom in chapter 24, the defense of God's righteousness in 15:11–18:14 and 39:12–35, and the praise of the Creator in 42:15–43:33) suggests that the author composed his book in stages from school texts. The autobiographical comments in 24:30–34; 31(34):12; and 39:12, 32 offer indications of his redactional activity. Furthermore, the two colophons in 50:27–29 and 51:30c–e (H^B) suggest that the psalm of Ben Sira in 50:1–30b was only secondarily appended to the book.

Comment 8: Inclusion of School Traditions? The problem of the extent to which Ben Sira composed the school texts himself or (as seems likely at least for 24:1–22 in view of the abrupt new beginning in v. 23) appropriated them from wisdom school materials requires further investigation.[23]

---

[21] Skehan and Di Lella, AB 39, xiii–xvi, offer an extensive analysis listing the individual themes treated and a catalog of themes (4–5). For Ben Sira's ethical doctrine, see also Collins, *Jewish Wisdom*, 62–79.

[22] See Marböck, *Gottes Weisheit*, 76–77.

[23] On the problem of secondary insertions, see Middendorp, *Stellung*, 113–36.

Issue 6: Judaism and Hellenism in Ben Sira. A series of themes new in Jewish wisdom mirror Ben Sira's situation, defined by the encounter with Hellenism. To these may be added a whole series of motifs with parallels in Greek literature and philosophy.[24] Ben Sira employed them in interpreting the biblical tradition without abandoning Jewish monotheism and the ethic of decision anchored in Deuteronomy. For him, obedience to the Torah remains the source of wisdom, and the fear of the Lord its root and crown. In the Praise of the Fathers he employed the Greek form of the encomium in order to convince his students that they could look back with pride on their own past in which God had led Israel until their own times through those he had called.

Comment 9: The Themes of the Didactic Texts That Suggest the Hellenistic Setting. Under the influence of Hellenistic culture, Ben Sira either introduced or newly accented a preexisting series of themes. This includes at least his recommendation of the physician in 38:1–15,[25] his admonitions regarding proper behavior at a banquet in 34(31):12–35(32):13,[26] and presumably also the significance he attributes to honor and shame (3:16; 4:20–31; 10:19–25; and 20:21–23).[27] His assumption in 39:4 that a *sofer* or scribe obviously takes journeys solely in order to become acquainted with the practices of foreign nations (see also 31[34]:9–13) cannot be understood apart from the broadened horizons resulting from contact with Hellenistic culture.[28] His basically conservative attitude apparently did not hinder him from adopting lifestyles and patterns of behavior that seemed wise and proper to him in his teaching. At the same time, the theme of

---

[24] On the possible influences of late Egyptian wisdom, see J. T. Sanders, *Ben Sira and Demotic Wisdom* (SBLMS 28; Chico: Scholars Press, 1983); and, similarly, Collins, *Jewish Wisdom*, 40–41. It is plausible that echoes are probably the result of a gnomic Koine that developed in the eastern Mediterranean in the second half of the first century B.C.E. and a common Hellenistic viewpoint; see M. Lichtheim, *Late Egyptian Wisdom in the International Context* (OBO 52; Göttingen: Vandenhoeck & Ruprecht, 1983), 185–86. Regarding the comparison with Menander, see C. Wildberg, "Ursprung, Function, und Inhalt der Weisheit bei Jesus Sirach und in den Sentenzen der Menander" (M.Th. thesis, University of Marburg, 1985).

[25] See J. Marböck, *Weisheit im Wandel: Untersuchungen zur Weisheitstheologie bei Ben Sira* (BBB 37; Bonn: Hanstein, 1971 [= 2d ed.; BZAW 272; New York: de Gruyter, 1999], 154–60; D. Lührmann, "Aber auch dem Arzt gib Raum (Sir 38,1–15)," *WD* 15 (1979): 55–78; Wischmeyer, *Kultur*, 46–48; H. Avalos, *Illness and Health Care in the Ancient Near East* (HSM 54; Atlanta: Scholars Press, 1995), 294–95.

[26] See Marböck, *Weisheit im Wandel*, 162–64; Wischmeyer, *Kultur*, 106–9; Collins, *Jewish Wisdom*, 32–33; and H.-V. Kieweler, "Benehmen bei Tisch," in *Der Einzelne* (ed. Egger-Wenzel and Krammer), 191–215.

[27] Collins, *Jewish Wisdom*, 34–35.

[28] Marböck, *Weisheit im Wandel*, 161–62; and Wischmeyer, *Kultur*, 96–97.

friendship, developed in an unusually broad manner in comparison to previous Jewish wisdom, mirrors the fragility of natural ties one often finds in times of change (6:5–17; 7:18; 9:10; 11:29–34; 12:8–9; 22:19–26; 27:16–21; 33:6; and 37:1–15).[29]

Comment 10: Greek Motifs and Their Incorporation into the Thought of Ben Sira. In 175 B.C.E. the high priest Jason obtained permission from Antiochus IV to found a Polis Antiocheia in Jerusalem and to establish the associated educational institutions of the gymnasium and the *ephebie* (2 Macc 4:9). This shows that the Jewish upper class in Jerusalem in the first decades of the second century B.C.E. had already experienced sufficient cultural contact with Hellenism to know what they were adopting. Consequently, it is no wonder that a whole series of motifs are also found in Ben Sira that he adopted from Greek literature (some perhaps also through oral means). Thus, for example, "before death, call no person fortunate" (Sir 11:28; H 11:26) has parallels in Herodotus, 1.32:7; 86:3, Sophocles, *Oed. tyr.* 1528–30, and Euripedes, *Andr.* 100–102, and the comparison of the changing of the generations with the shoots on a green tree in 14:18 finds its counterpart in Homer, *Iliad* 6.146.[30] Stoic influences on his thought prove to be theologically more significant.[31] When, in his hymn to God's providence in 39:12–35, Ben Sira praises God who surveys the course of the whole world (v. 20)[32] and whose providential and teleological activity in creation

---

[29] See F. V. Reiterer, ed., *Freundschaft bei Ben Sira* (BZAW 244; New York: de Gruyter, 1996); Collins, *Jewish Wisdom*, 40 and 74–75; and J. Corley, "Friendship according to Ben Sira," in *Der Einzelne* (ed. Egger-Wenzel and Krammer), 65–72; on the sociological background, see also O. Kaiser, "Lysis oder von der Freundschaft," *ZRGG* 32 (1980): 215–18 (= *Der Mensch unter dem Schicksal: Studien zur Geschichte, Theologie und Gegenwartsbedeutung der Weisheit* [BZAW 161; New York: de Gruyter, 1985], 228–31); O. Kaiser in *Freundschaft* (ed. Reiterer), 107 and 120–21 (= O. Kaiser, *Gottes und der Menschen Weisheit* [BZAW 261; New York: de Gruyter, 1998], 217 and 231–32).

[30] For further parallels, at least in the Greek gnomic poetry of Theognis, see O. Kaiser, "Judentum und Hellenismus: Ein Beitrag zur Frage nach dem hellenistischen Einfluß auf Kohelet und Jesus Sirach," *VF* 27 (1982): 68–86, esp. 82–83 (= O. Kaiser, *Der Mensch unter dem Schicksal*, 135–53, esp. 149–50); extensive treatment in H.-V. Kieweler, *Ben Sira zwischen Judentum und Hellenismus: Eine Auseinandersetzung mit Th. Middendorp* (BEATAJ 30; New York: Lang, 1992); furthermore, Collins, *Jewish Wisdom*, 32–41; and, as ever, M. Hengel, *Judaism and Hellenism*, 75–76.

[31] See R. Pautrel, "Ben Sira et le Stoïcisme," *RSR* 51 (1963): 535–49, who proceeds too broadly however. See O. Kaiser, "Die Rezeption der stoischen Providenz bei Ben Sira," *JNSL* 24 (1998): 1–14; and U. Wicke-Reuter, *Göttliche Providenz und menschliche Verantwortung bei Ben Sira und in der frühen Stoa* (BZAW 298; New York: de Gruyter, 2000).

[32] Regarding the—by no means pantheistic—significance of *hu' hakkol* ("He alone is all") in 43:27 as a description of his creative power, see Kaiser, "Rezeption," 9–10.

stands in the service of distributive justice (vv. 16–35; compare also 33:7–15),[33] dependence on the Stoic doctrine of the providence of Zeus is unmistakable. It is equally clear, however, that, in accordance with his postdeuteronomistic ethic of decision (15:11–20),[34] he avoids the concept of predestination associated with providence for the Stoics.[35] For him, the concept of God's providence and omniscience serves exclusively in defense of his omnipotent justice. Already at creation, God prepared the means to reward the good and punish the evil. Similarly, in 42:15–43:33, which concludes his teaching, he placed the notion of the harmonious beauty of the whole, a concept that traces back to Plato and that was developed by the Stoa, in the service of the glorification of the unfathomability of divine wisdom.[36] Where Ben Sirach appropriates Greek thought, he is not interested in eliminating traditional elements of ancestral religion but in thoughtfully interpreting them. The God of Abraham, Isaac, and Israel, and not the god of the philosophers, made his people party to hidden wisdom in the form of the Torah. In God's administration, Ben Sira perceives his prescience, omniscience, and providence.[37] If divine wisdom governs even the whole cosmos and all wisdom on earth stems in principle from God (Sir 1:1–10; 24:1–22),[38] then, for Ben Sira, the Torah given Moses by God himself was and remains the sum and source of wisdom (Sir 24:23–34; 45:5).[39] Its beginning, middle, and goal, however, consist in the fear of the Lord (Sir 1:10–30).[40] The wisdom that governs the world in a hidden fashion found its dwelling on earth in Jacob and on Zion (24:1–23*). It is communicated to those who fear God, who learn in the school of the Torah to control their impulses (Sir 21:11).

---

[33] Compare G. L. Prato, *Il problema della teodicea in Ben Sira: Composizione dei contrari e richiamo alle origini* (AnBib 65; Rome: Biblical Institute Press, 1975); Collins, *Jewish Wisdom*, 84–96; and Wicke-Reuter, *Göttliche Providenz*.

[34] See G. Maier, *Mensch und freier Wille: Nach den jüdischen Religionsparteien zwischen Ben Sira und Paulus* (WUNT 12; Tübingen: Mohr/Siebeck, 1971), 85–97.

[35] Contrast Maier, *Mensch*, 98–112, and a critique of Maier in Wicke-Reuter, *Göttliche Providenz*.

[36] See Kaiser, "Rezeption," 47–51.

[37] See also Kaiser, *GAT* II, 143–46.

[38] See Marböck, *Weisheit im Wandel*, 131–33.

[39] See Collins, *Jewish Wisdom*, 42–61.

[40] Regarding its aspects, see J. Haspecker, *Gottesfurcht bei Jesus Sirach: Ihre religiöse Struktur und ihre literarische und doktrinäre Bedeutung* (AnBib; Rome: Pontifical Biblical Institute, 1967).

Bibliography

Bibliography (1475–1998):
F. V. Reiterer et al. *Bibliographie zu Ben Sira.* BZAW 266. New York: de Gruyter, 1998.

Introduction:
Steuernagel. *Einleitung,* 792–95.
Oesterley. *Introduction,* 222–55.
Eißfeldt. *Introduction,* 595–99.
Schürer/Vermes 3.1:198–212.
T. Kluser et al., eds. *Reallexikon für Antike und Christentum.* Stuttgart: Hiersemann, 1995, 134: 878–906.
J. Marböck. "Das Buch Jesus Sirach." Pages 363–70 in Zenger, *Einleitung.*
R. E. Murphy, *The Tree of Life: An Exploration of Biblical Wisdom Literature.* 2d ed. Grand Rapids: Eerdmans, 1996.
J. J. Collins. *Jewish Wisdom,* 23–96.
R. J. Coggins. *Sirach.* Guides to Apocrypha and Pseudepigrapha. Sheffield: Sheffield Academic Press, 1998.

Histories of Research:
P. C. Beentjes. "Recent Publications on the Wisdom of Jesus ben Sira (Ecclesiasticus)." *Bijdr* 43 (1978): 260–65.
F. V. Reiterer. "Review of Recent Research on the Book of Ben Sira (1980–1996)." Pages 23–60 in *The Book of Ben Sira in Modern Research: Proceedings of the First International Ben Sira Conference, 28–31 July 1996, Soesterberg, Netherlands.* Edited by P. C. Beentjes. BZAW 255. New York: de Gruyter, 1997.

Editions of the Text:

Greek:

J. Ziegler, ed. *Sapientia Iesu filii Sirach, Septuaginta.* 2d ed. Vetus Testamentum graece auctoritate Academiae Scientiarum Gottingensis editum XII/2. Göttingen: Vandenhoeck & Ruprecht, 1980.

Hebrew:

P. C. Beentjes, ed. *The Book of Ben Sira in Hebrew: A Text Edition of all Extant Hebrew Manuscripts and A Synopsis of All Parallel Hebrew Ben Sira Texts.* VTSup 68. Leiden: Brill, 1997.

Syriac:

P. A. de Lagarde, ed. *Libri Veteris Testamenti apocryphi syriace.* Leipzig: Brockhaus, 1861. Repr., Osnabrück: Zeller, 1972.

Latin:

R. Weber, ed. *Biblia Sacra iuxta vulgatam versionem II.* Stuttgart: Wurttembergische Bibelanstalt, 1975. Pages 1029–95.

W. Thiele. *Vetus Latina.* Die Reste der altlateinischen Bibel 11.1. Freiburg: Herder, 1985–1987.

Polyglot:

F. Vattioni. *Ecclesiatico: Testo ebraico con apparato critico e versioni greca, latina e siriaca.* Pubblicazioni del Seminario di Semitistica. Testi 1. Naples: Instituto Orientale di Napoli, 1968.

Other Editions of the Text:

S. Schechter and C. Taylor, eds. *The Wisdom of Ben Sira: Portions of the Book of Ecclesiasticus: Hebrew Text Ed. from Hebrew Manuscripts in the Cairo Geniza Collection Presented to the University of Cambridge by the Editors.* Cambridge: Cambridge University Press, 1899. Repr., Amsterdam: APA-Philo Press, 1979.

H. L. Strack. *Die Sprüche Jesus', des Sohnes Sirachs: Der jüngst gefundene hebräische Text mit Anmerkungen und Wörterbuch.* SIJB 31. Leipzig: Deichert, 1903.

I. Levi, *The Hebrew Text of the Book of Ecclesiasticus, Edited with Brief Notes and a Selected Glossary.* SSS 3. Leiden: Brill, 1904.

R. Smend. *Die Weisheit des Jesus Sirach, hebräisch und deutsch.* Berlin: Reimer, 1906.

J. Marcus. *The Newly Discovered Original Hebrew of Ben Sira (Ecclesiasticus XXXII.16–XXXIV,1): The Fifth Manuscript and a Prosodic Version of Ben Sira (Ecclesiasticus XXII,2–XXIII,9).* Philadelphia: Dropsie College for Hebrew and Cognate Learning, 1931.

M. H. Segal. *Seper Ben Sira Haschalem.* 2d ed. Jerusalem: Mosad Byalik, 1958.

Biblia Sacra iuxta latinam vulgatam versionem cura et studio monachorum Abbatiae Pontificiae S. Hieronymi in Urbe O.S.B. edita XII. Rome: Typis Polyglottis Vaticanis, 1964.

J. A. Sanders. *The Psalms Scroll of Qumran Cave 11 (11QPsᵃ).* DJD 4. Oxford: Clarendon, 1965.

Y. Yadin. *Ben Sira Scroll from Masada, with Introduction, Emendations and Commentary.* Jerusalem: Israel Exploration Society, 1965.

————. "The Ben Sira Scroll from Masada: With Notes on the Reading by Elisha Qimron and Bibliography by Florentino García Martínez." Pages 151–252 in *Masada VI: Yigael Yadin Excavations 1963–1965, Final Reports*. Edited by Shemaryahu Talmon et al. Jerusalem: Israel Exploration Society, 1999.

Studies on the Text and the History of the Text:

A. A. Di Lella. *The Hebrew Text of Sirach: A Text-Critical and Historical Study*. The Hague: Mouton, 1966.

H.-P. Rüger. *Text und Textform im hebräischen Sirach: Eine Untersuchung zur Textgeschichte und Textkritik der hebräischen Sirachfragmente aus der Kairoer Geniza*. BZAW 112. New York: de Gruyter, 1970.

O. Wahl. *Der Sirach-Text der Sacra parallela*. FB 16. Würzburg: Echter, 1974.

M. M. Winter. "The Origins of Ben Sira in Syriac (Part I)." *VT* 27 (1977): 237–53.

————. "The Origins of Ben Sira in Syriac (Part II)." *VT* 27 (1977): 494–507.

F. V. Reiterer. *"Urtext" und Übersetzungen: Sprachstudie über Sir 44,16–45,26 als Beitrag zur Sirachforschung*. ATS 12. St. Ottilien: EOS Verlag, 1980.

M. D. Nelson. *The Syriac Version of the Wisdom of Ben Sira Compared to the Greek and Hebrew Materials*. SBLDS 107. Atlanta: Scholars Press, 1988.

R. J. Owens. "The Early Syriac Text of Ben Sira in the Demonstrations of Aphrahat." *JSS* 34 (1989): 39–75.

B. G. Wright. *No Small Difference: Sirach's Relationship to Its Hebrew Parent Text*. SBLSCS 26. Atlanta: Scholars Press, 1989.

K. W. Samaan. *Sept traductions arabes de Ben Sira*. EHST 492. New York: Lang, 1994.

A. Minissale. *La versione greca del Siracide: Confronto con il testo ebraico alla luce dell'attività midrascica e del metodo targumico*. AnBib 133. Rome: Pontifical Biblical Institute, 1995.

St. C. Reif. "The Discovery of the Cambridge Genizah Fragments of Ben Sira: Scholars and Texts." Pages 1–22 in *The Book of Ben Sira in Modern Research: Proceedings of the First Annual Ben Sira Conference, 28–31 July 1996*. Edited by P. C. Beentjes. BZAW 255. New York: de Gruyter, 1997.

C. Martone. "The Ben Sira Manuscripts from Qumran and Masada." Pages 81–94 in *The Book of Ben Sira in Modern Research: Proceedings of the First Annual Ben Sira Conference, 28–31 July 1996*. Edited by P. C. Beentjes. BZAW 255. New York: de Gruyter, 1997.

Chr. Wagner. *Die Septuaginta-Hapaxlegomena im Buch Jesus Sirach: Unter-suchungen zu Wortwahl und Wortbildung unter besonderer Berück-sichtigung des textkritischen und übersetzungstechnischen Aspekts.* BZAW 282. New York: de Gruyter, 1999.

Aids:
R. Smend. *Griechisch-Syrisch-Hebräischer Index zur Weisheit des Jesus Sirach.* Berlin: Reimer, 1907.
D. Barthélmy and O. Rickenbacher. *Konkordanz zum hebräischen Sirach: Mit syrisch-hebräischem Index.* Göttingen: Vandenhoeck & Ruprecht, 1973.
M. M. Winter. *A Concordance to the Peshitta Version of Ben Sira.* MPIL 2. Leiden: Brill, 1976.

Issues:
W. Baumgartner. "Die literarischen Gattungen in der Weisheit des Jesus Sirach." *ZAW* 34 (1914): 161–98.
J. Fichtner. *Die altorientalische Weisheit in ihrer israelitisch-jüdischen Aus-prägung: Eine Studie zur Nationalisierung der Weisheit in Israel.* BZAW 62. Gießen: Töpelmann, 1933.
V. Hamp. "Zukunft und Jenseits im Buche Sirach." Pages 86–97 in *Alttesta-mentliche Studien: FS F. Nötscher.* Edited by H. Junker and J. Botter-weck. BBB 1. Bonn: Hanstein, 1950.
V. Tcherikover. *Hellenistic Civilization and the Jews.* Translated by S. Apple-baum. New York: JPS, 1961.
E. G. Bauckmann. "Die Proverbien und die Sprüche des Jesus Sirach: Eine Untersuchung zum Strukturwandel der israelitischen Weisheitslehre." *ZAW* 72 (1960): 33–63.
R. Pautrel. "Ben Sira et le stoïcisme." *RSR* 51 (1963): 535–49.
H. Conzelmann. "Die Mutter der Weisheit." Pages 225–34 in *Zeit und Geschichte: FS R. Bultmann.* Edited by E. Dinkler. Tübingen: Mohr, 1964.
J. Haspecker. *Gottesfurcht bei Jesus Sirach: Ihre religiöse Struktur und ihre literarische und doktrinäre Bedeutung.* AnBib 30. Rome: Pontifical Bib-lical Institute, 1967.
M. Hengel. *Judaism and Hellenism.* Philadelphia: Fortress, 1974.
G. von Rad, "Die Weisheit des Jesus Sirach." *EvT* 24 (1969): 113–33.
G. Maier. *Mensch und freier Wille: Nach den jüdischen Religionsparteien zwischen Ben Sira und Paulus.* WUNT 12. Tübingen: Mohr/Siebeck, 1971.
J. Marböck. *Weisheit im Wandel: Untersuchungen zur Weisheitstheologie bei Ben Sira.* BBB 37. Bonn: Hanstein, 1971. 2d ed. with appendix and bibliography, BZAW 272. New York: de Gruyter, 1999.
———, *Gottes Weisheit unter uns: Zur Theologie des Buches Sirach.* HBS 6. New York: Herder, 1995.

————, "Structure and Redaction History in the Book of Ben Sira (1960–1996)." Pages 23–60 in *The Book of Ben Sira in Modern Research: Proceedings of the First International Ben Sira Conference, 28–31 July 1966.* Edited by P. C. Beentjes. BZAW 255. New York: de Gruyter, 1997.

T. Middendorp. *Die Stellung Jesu Ben Siras zwischen Judentum und Hellenismus.* Leiden: Brill, 1973.

O. Rickenbacher. *Weisheitsperikopen bei Ben Sira.* OBO 1. Göttingen: Vandenhoeck & Ruprecht, 1973.

J. L. Crenshaw. "The Problem of Theodicy in Sirach: On Human Bondage." *JBL* 94 (1975): 47–64.

G. L. Prato. *Il problema della teodicea in Ben Sira: Composizione dei contrari e richiamo alle origini.* AnBib 65. Rome: Biblical Institute Press, 1975.

D. Lührmann. "Aber auch dem Arzt gib Raum (Sir 38,1–15)." *WD* 15 (1979): 55–78.

H. Stadelmann. *Ben Sira als Schriftgelehrter: Eine Untersuchung zum Berufsbild des vor-makkabäischen Sofer unter Berücksichtigung seines Verhältnisses zu Priester-, Prophethen- und Weisheitslehrtum.* WUNT 2.6. Tübingen: Mohr/Siebeck, 1980.

K. Bringmann. *Hellenistische Reform und Religionsverfolgung: Eine Untersuchung zur jüdisch-hellenistischen Geschichte (175–165 v.Chr.).* AAWG 3.132. Göttingen: Vandenhoeck & Ruprecht, 1983.

J. T. Sanders. *Ben Sira and Demotic Wisdom.* SBLMS 28. Chico: Scholars Press, 1983.

O. Kaiser. *Der Mensch unter dem Schicksal: Studien zur Geschichte, Theologie und Gegenwartsbedeutung der Weisheit.* BZAW 161. New York: de Gruyter, 1985.

————. *Gottes und des Menschen Weisheit.* BZAW 261. New York: de Gruyter, 1998.

————. "Die Rezeption der stoischen Providenz bei Ben Sira: Memorial F. Deist." *JNSL* 24 (1998): 1–14.

————. "Der Mensch als Geschöpf Gottes: Aspekte der Anthropolgie Ben Siras." Pages 1–22 in *Der Einzelne und seine Gemeinschaft bei Ben Sira.* Edited by R. Egger-Wenzel and R. Krammer. BZAW 270. New York: de Gruyter, 1998.

E. J. Schnabel. *Law and Wisdom from Ben Sira to Paul: A Tradition historical Enquiry into the Relation of Law, Wisdom, and Ethics.* WUNT 2.16. Tübingen: Mohr, 1985.

C. Wildberg. "Ursprung, Funktion und Inhalt der Weisheit bei Jesus Sirach und in den Sentenzen des Menander." M.Th. thesis, University of Marburg, 1985.

T. R. Lee. *Studies in the Form of Sirach 44–50.* SBLDS 75. Chico: Scholars Press, 1986.

H. V. Kieweler. *Ben Sira zwischen Judentum und Hellenismus: Eine Auseinandersetzung mit Th. Middendorp.* BEATAJ 30. New York: Lang, 1992.

L. Schrader. *Leiden und Gerechtigkeit: Studien zu Theologie und Textgeschichte des Sirachbuches.* BBET 27. New York: Lang, 1994.

R. A. Argall. *I Henoch and Sirach: A Comparative Literary and Conceptional Analysis of the Themes of Revelation, Creation and Judgement.* SBLEJL 8. Atlanta: Scholars Press, 1995.

O. Wischmeyer. *Die Kultur des Buches Jesus Sirach.* BZNW 77. New York: de Gruyter, 1995.

J. I. Okoye. *Speech in Ben Sira with Special Reference to 5,9–6,1.* EHST 535. New York: Lang, 1996.

R. E. Murphy. *The Tree of Life: An Exploration of Biblical Wisdom Literature.* 2d ed. Grand Rapids: Eerdmans, 1996.

F. V. Reiterer, ed. *Freundschaft bei Ben Sira.* BZAW 244. New York: de Gruyter, 1996.

P. C. Beentjes, ed. *The Book of Ben Sira in Modern Research.* BZAW 255. New York: de Gruyter, 1997.

J. J. Collins. *Jewish Wisdom in the Hellenistic Age.* Louisville: Westminster John Knox, 1997.

U. Wicke-Reuter, *Göttliche Providenz und menschliche Verantwortung bei Ben Sira und in der frühen Stoa.* BZAW 298. New York: de Gruyter, 2000.

Commentaries:
V. Ryssel, *APAT,* 1900; R. Smend, EK, 1906; G. H. Box and W. O. F. Oesterley, *APOT,* 1913; N. Peters, EHAT, 1913; P. Volz, SAT, 1921²; A. Eberharter, HSAT, 1925; V. Hamp, EB, 1955; J. Snaith, CBC, 1974; G. Sauer, *JSHRZ,* 1980; P. Skehan and A. A. Di Lella, AB, 1987; A. A. Di Lella, NJBC, 1991; G. Sauer, ATD, 2000.

Wisdom of Solomon

Thesis 1: Intention and Age of the Document. The deuterocanonical Wisdom of Solomon is a commendation of the Jewish religion in a Hellenistic environment. Its dating varies in the current discussion between the last third of the second century B.C.E. and the middle of the first century C.E. Yet there are good grounds to date it no earlier than the final third of the first century B.C.E. Based on the references in 7:7–8 and 9:7–8, the

Greek superscription of the book as well as translations of it refer to Solomon as the author.

Issue 1: The Name of the Book. Superscriptions in the Greek or Latin manuscripts designate the book *Sophia Salomonis* or *Sapientia Salomonis*, that is, Wisdom of Solomon or briefly *Sapientia*, or Wisdom. It owes this designation to its ostensible function as the exhortation of a king to his fellow rulers to seek righteousness and wisdom (Wis 1:1; 6:1–2; and 6:21–24). The speaker claims this wisdom for himself as a gift granted him by God in response to his prayer (7:7–14, 15–20). His affirmation in 7:8 that he prefers wisdom to scepters and thrones and his report in 7:15–30 that he received it in abundance from God (see 1 Kgs 3:4–9; 5:9–12; 10:1–5) are supposed to elicit his identification as King Solomon. The confession placed in his mouth in 9:7–8 that God chose him as the king of his people (1 Kgs 3:6–7) and commissioned him to build the temple and the altar (2 Sam 7:12–13; 1 Kgs 8:15–21; see also 1 Chr 22:6–19) serves the same purpose. With this fiction, the unknown author of the book continues in a fashion surpassing his predecessors the late Old Testament tradition of subordinating Jewish wisdom literature, such as Proverbs, Qoheleth, and the Song of Solomon, to Solomonic authority.[41]

Thesis 2: Its Literary Character, Structure, and Intention. In 1:1 (compare 6:1, 21), the book addresses the kings of the earth in imitation of the Hellenistic literary genre "concerning the monarchy." It challenges them to love justice and to seek the Lord in simplicity of heart. The other themes treated justify the assumption that the actual, though not necessarily the exclusive, addressees were Jews who were versed both in Judaism as well as in Hellenistic culture. By means of the contrast between formal and real addressees, between the fictive situation in which King Solomon speaks to world leaders and the real situation of the middle-class Jewish reader, the latter is placed at a distance that challenges him or her to adopt the author's own position and, finally, allows him or her to identify with the "we" that confesses to God in the third section (12:6,18,22; 15:1–3,4 and 18:8).[42]

The document divides into three sections: (1) the exhortation in 1:1–6:21, which calls for the love of justice and promises in reward the gift of eternal life; (2) the praise of wisdom in 6:22–11:1; and (3) a laudatory

---

[41] See also D. G. Meade, *Pseudonymity and Canon: An Investigation into the Relationship of Authorship and Authority in Jewish and Earliest Christian Tradition* (WUNT 39; Tübingen: Mohr, 1986), 62–66.

[42] H. Engel, NSKAT 16, 25–27.

reminiscence of the divine deliverance of Israel from Egypt and its guidance through the wilderness in the form of seven antitheses documenting divine justice.

Regarding the appropriate genre designation for the Greek version of the book, James M. Reese seems correct, despite its partial stylization according to the pattern of Hellenistic essays concerning the monarchy, in treating it as a *protreptikos*, that is, as a propaganda pamphlet for Jewish wisdom rooted in obedience to the Torah.[43]

Issue 2: The Structure of the Book. The book divides easily into three major sections:

1:1–6:21   An exhortation to a life in justice and wisdom in view of the fate of the pious and the godless

6:22–11:1   Commendation of wisdom

6:22–9:19 The praise of wisdom

(9:1–18 Solomon's prayer for wisdom)

10:1–11:1 Seven examples of the delivering power of wisdom

11:2–19:22   Seven antitheses or analogies of God's punishment of Israel's enemies and deliverance of Israel

Insertion 1: God's manner of punishment (11:15–12:27)

Insertion 2: The folly of idolatry (13:1–15:19)

A heptadic scheme appears to shape, in different ways, the first, second, and third portions. Thus the exhortation comprising the first section is shaped according to a concentric, heptadic step pattern. Verses 10:1–11:1 in the second section offer seven examples of the delivering power of wisdom in the time from Adam to Israel's journey through the wilderness. The third section contains seven antitheses, termed *syncrises* in Attic rhetoric, from Israel's history for God's punishment of the enemies and deliverance of Israel. In contrast, verses 6:22–9:19 display a concentric, pentadic step pattern.

---

[43] J. M. Reese, *Hellenistic Influence on the Book of Wisdom and Its Consequences* (AnBib 41; Rome: Pontifical Biblical Institute, 1970), 117–21; and on the discussion, J. J. Collins, *Jewish Wisdom in the Hellenistic Age* (Louisville: Westminster John Knox, 1997), 179–82; Engel, NSKAT 16, 25–28; and M. Kepper, *Hellenistische Bildung im Buch der Weisheit: Studien zur Sprachgestalt und Theologie der Sapientia Salomonis* (BZAW 280; New York: de Gruyter, 1999).

Comment 1: Rhetorical Style. The poetry of the Wisdom of Solomon employs the *parallelismus membrorum* typical of Semitic poetry, which as a
rule is bipartite and occasionally tripartite, and which is apparent in the
antithetically, synonymously, or in its analytical form, synthetically bal-
anced cola or lines. Occasional monocola function to summarize or
emphasize. In addition, Hellenistic rhetoric has effectively influenced
Wisdom.[44] Thus, *litotes* or understated simplicity (see, for example, 1:2)
and *paronomasia* or wordplay (see, for example, 12:25) appear. According
to J. M. Reese,[45] the sprung word placement of the *hyperbaton*, in which
the attributive is separated from its referent by another word, appears 240
times (see, for example, 9:4), so that, without an understanding of this
form, the text often appears to be senseless. Additional literary techniques
include the summary chain or *sorites* (see 6:17–21); *anaphora* or a series of
similar words (see 13:17–19); *catalogue-like lists* (for example, 7:22–23) as
an intensification of the often employed *heptadic series* (see 7:8–10;
10:1–21; and 11:2–19:22); *inclusios* (compare, for example, 1:1a with
1:15); keywords emphasizing the content of a section (see, for example,
"thirst" and "to thirst" in 11:4–14); chains of keywords (compare, for example, 1:10 with 1:11); themes foreshadowed at the end of the preceding
section (see 1:11–15); and cross references concluding minor sections (see,
for example, vv. 8c and 10a in 12:8b–11).[46]

Thesis 3: The Author. The author enjoyed a Judeo-Hellenistic education
that equipped him both to handle biblical and extrabiblical Jewish literature in superior allusions as well as to employ the language of late Hellenistic culture and its stylistic techniques. He also assumes a corresponding
literacy on the part of his readers. Consequently, he is to be located in a bi-
lingual Judaism with a corresponding educational system, such as is attested for the Jewish *politeuma* of Alexandria.

Thesis 4: Significance for the History of Religion and Theology. The contribution of the author consists in the fact that, with the diction of Greek
rhetoric and elements of Hellenistic, especially Stoic, philosophy, he portrayed the rationality of belief in a God superior to the world and all its

---

[44] See E. Focke, *Die Entstehung der Weisheit Salomos: Ein Beitrag zur Geschichte des
jüdischen Hellenismus* (FRLANT 22; Göttingen: Vandenhoeck & Ruprecht, 1913), 55–65.

[45] J. M. Reese, *Hellenistic Influence,* 26–27; see also D. Winston, AB 43, 15; and the
analyses by A. G. Wright, "The Structure of the Book of Wisdom," *Bib* 48 (1967): 165–84;
and on the numerical patterns, A. G. Wright, "Numerical Patterns in the Book of Wisdom," *CBQ* 29 (1967): 524–38.

[46] See Reese, *Hellenistic Influence,* 25–31; Engel, NSKAT 16, 15–19; and Kepper,
Hellenistische Bildung.

powers and in God's righteousness manifest in the bestowal of eternal life on the righteous and the condemnation of the evildoers in the Last Judgment (13:1–8). Furthermore, his contribution testifies to the development of the Judeo-Hellenistic speculative wisdom between Prov 8–9, Ben Sira, and Philo. During the course of this development, wisdom increasingly acquired cosmological and hypostatic features under the influence first of Isis aretalogies and then of the Stoic and mid-Platonic concept of the Logos and the world soul.

Issue 3: Position in the Canon. Since the book was originally composed in Greek and despite its subordination to the authority of Solomon, it was excluded from the rabbinic Bible. The Septuagint situates it between Job and Sirach, the Vulgate between Song of Songs and Sirach. Even if the apostle Paul did not use it in Rom 1:18–32, he must have had access to an exemplar related to Wis 13:1–9.[47] The book enjoyed increasing popularity in the early church.[48] The Muratorian Canon (ll. 69–70) even included it expressly among the New Testament writings.[49] Otherwise, however, its appropriate placement in the Old Testament held sway. The Roman Catholic and Greek Orthodox churches consider the book deuterocanonical. Following Luther's (as before him Jerome's) judgment in favor of the canon of the Hebrew Bible, Protestant churches count it among the Apocrypha. Among them, the Wisdom of Solomon finds its place in the Luther Bible between Judith and Sirach.

---

[47] See, most recently, N. Walter, "Sapientia Salomonis und Paulus: Bericht über eine Hallenser Dissertation von Paul-Gerhard Keyser aus dem Jahre 1971," in *Die Weisheit Salomos im Horizont biblischer Theologie* (ed. H. Hübner; BThSt 22; Neukirchen-Vluyn: Neukirchener Verlag, 1993), 93–99, who considers essentially apropos the evidence introduced by H. Grafe ("Das Verhältnis der paulinischen Schriften zur Sapientia Salomonis," in *Theologische Abhandlungen: FS C. von Weizsäcker* [ed. A. von Harnack et al.; Freiburg: Mohr/Siebeck, 1892], 251–86) that Paul knew Wisdom. P.-G. Keyser ("Sapientia Salomonis und Paulus: Eine Analyse der Sapientia Salomonis und ein Vergleich ihrer theologischen und anthropologischen Probleme mit denen des Paulus im Römerbrief" [PhD diss., University of Halle, 1971]) calls attention to the extensive analogies between Wisdom and Romans. His contention (230–31), that Wisdom is pluralistic, not only in the sense that it addresses various groups of readers, but also in the sense that it employs various interpretive keys to characterize analogous or identical content without explicating the relationship between the two, deserves particular attention. A systematic assessment of Wisdom must take this finding into account and will, accordingly, result in an open-ended portrayal.

[48] See C. Larcher, *Études sur le livre de la Sagesse* (EBib; Paris: Gabalda, 1969), 36–63; and now also J. I. Pock, *Hieronymus' Exegese des Weisheitsbuches im Licht der Tradition* (Dissertationen der Karl-Franzens-Universität Graz 89; Graz: Verlag für die Technische Universität Graz, 1992).

[49] See B. M. Metzger, *The Canon of the New Testament: Its Origin, Development, and Significance* (New York: Oxford University Press, 1987), 199 and 307.

Comment 2: Linguistic Indicators of the Date.[50] Linguistically, Wisdom displays the greatest number of *hapax legomena* in the Greek Bible and a significant proportion of them in comparison to Greek literature as a whole. It thus occupies a special place within the Septuagint, apparently as the latest book. In addition to the direct citations, the abundant use of biblical formulae indicates that the Septuagint influenced the book. Apart from this, its Greek vocabulary mirrors the late Hellenistic literary language, especially as expressed by the tragedians. The formation of its vocabulary also betrays the late Hellenistic period. A whole series of words is not otherwise attested before the first century C.E. Only incipient stages of the Atticist purification of the extravagant style, described as Asian, undertaken during the course of the first century C.E. have influenced the book. This purification is evident especially in the combination of vowels and the endings and beginnings of words (a phenomenon termed *hiatus*) dispersed throughout the whole document (see, for example, the concentration of them in 2:4). The terms *diagnōsis* ("judgment") in 3:18 and *kratēsis* ("dominion") in 6:3 have special significance. According to the suggestion of Giuseppe Scarpat,[51] with the cautious support of David Winston[52] and Martina Kepper,[53] they are probably employed in the sense of the official Augustan usage. The first served as a technical term in the court of appeals established by Augustus on his entry to office, the second for the Roman senate to designate the beginning of his rule in 26 B.C.E. Thus, as a whole, the linguistic evidence speaks for dating the document no earlier than the final third of the first century B.C.E.[54]

Comment 3: The Fate of the Righteous and the Godless: Structure and Content of 1:1–6:21.

A₁ 1:1–15   First exhortation of the judges of the earth to a God-oriented life that will not provoke their deaths

---

[50] See Kepper, *Hellenistische Bildung*, section II.

[51] G. Scarpat, "Ancora sulla data di compositione del libro della Sapienza," *RivB* 15 (1967): 171–89; G. Scarpat, "Ancora sulla data di compositione della Sapientia Salomonis," *RivB* 36 (1988): 363–75.

[52] Winston, AB 43, 153.

[53] Kepper, *Hellenistische Bildung*, 2.1.3–4.

[54] The appeal to 2:1–20 in support of a date in the period of the anti-Jewish pogrom in Alexandria in the time of Claudius Caesar, made by Winston (AB 43, 23), rests on a misperception of the text (see Collins, *Jewish Wisdom*, 179, 194–95). It does not relate to specific historical events but argues philosophically, as it were. Similarly, the appeal to 19:13–17 made most recently by S. Cheon (*The Exodus Story in the Wisdom of Solomon: A Study in Biblical Interpretation* [JSPSup 23; Sheffield: Sheffield Academic Press, 1997], 145–49) rests on the misperception of the paradigmatic character of the text.

B₁ 1:16–2:24 The disdain and persecution of the righteous as a result of the error of the godless

(C₁ 2:1–20 First speech of the godless)

D₁ 3:1–12 First refutation: The immortality of the righteous

D₂ 3:13–4:6 Second refutation: The lot of the childless but righteous woman

D₃ 4:7–19 Third refutation: The lot of the righteous who dies in
his youth[55]

B₂ 4:20–5:23 The delayed insight of the godless in the Last
Judgment

(C₂ 5:4–13 Second speech of the godless)

A₂ 6:1–21 Second exhortation to the kings of the earth to strive
for wisdom: Observance of its commandments as-
sures immortality and dominion[56]

The structure of this great exhortation introducing the book is
thoroughly dramatic.[57] Besides the pertinent prophetic texts (and here
especially Isa 52:13–62:2), other eschatological concepts such as have
been recorded in *1 Enoch,* and here, especially in the Book of Watchers
(*1 Enoch* 1–36)[58] and in the Letter of Enoch (*1 Enoch* 91–105:1),[59] stand
in the background of the characterization of the deeds and consequences of the righteous and their opponents, the evildoers or the
godless.[60]

---

[55] See also A. Schmitt, *Entrückung, Aufnahme, Himmelfahrt: Untersuchungen zu einem
Vorstellungsbereich im Alten Testament* (2d ed.; FB 10; Würzburg: Echter, 1976), 181–92.

[56] When v. 18 maintains that love consists in keeping the laws of wisdom, the Jewish
reader is supposed to hear echoes of Deut 10:11–12. The laws of wisdom are, indeed, the
laws of God.

[57] See the treatment by A. Schmitt, *Wende des Lebens: Untersuchungen zu einem Situations-Motiv der Bibel* (BZAW 237; New York: de Gruyter, 1996), 20–48.

[58] On the age of the book, see F. García Martínez, *Qumran and Apocalyptic: Studies on
the Aramaic Texts from Qumran* (STDJ 9; Leiden: Brill, 1992), 60–72, esp. 71–72.

[59] On the problem of the delimitation of this unit, see García Martínez, *Qumran and
Apocalyptic,* 79–96.

[60] See J. Fichtner, "Die Stellung der Sapientia Salomonis in der Literatur- und
Geistesgeschichte ihrer Zeit," *ZNW* 36 (1937): 113–32 and esp. 124–32; P. Grelot, "L'eschatologie de la Sagesse et les apocalypses juives," in *A la rencontre de Dieu: Mémorial A. Gelin*
(ed. M. Jourjon et al.; Bibliothèque de la Faculté de Théologie de Lyon 8; Le Puy: Mappus,
1961), 165–78; Larcher, *Études,* 103–12; and Collins, *Jewish Wisdom,* 183–85.

Comment 4: The Commendation of Wisdom and the Report of the Search for Wisdom. The Structure of 6:22–9:1:8.

A₁ 6:22–25   Declaration of the intention to reveal its secret

B₁ 7:1–22a   Autobiographical report of God's gift of universal wisdom

C 7:22b–8:1   The praise of wisdom as the reflection of the character and goodness of God that penetrates and illuminates all minds

B₂ 8:2–21   Autobiographical report of the search for wisdom as the creator of the universe

A₂ 9:1–18   Prayer to the creator of the universe to grant wisdom as an aid in the recognition of his will

This description of the contents already reveals that the personalization of wisdom in Wisdom of Solomon has been further intensified in comparison to her role in Sirach. A comparison of the statements made concerning her and concerning God himself shows that the figure of wisdom still waivers between a personification and a hypostasis.[61] In terms of the history of religion, her role seems to have been influenced by that of the Egyptian goddess Isis, who, as the daughter of the sun god Re, consort of King Osiris, and mother of Horus, prefigures the concept of the special relationship of wisdom to God and to the king (compare 8:3 with 8:9).[62] In terms of the history of philosophy, wisdom's role as mediator between God and the world corresponds to efforts encountered in Eudoros of Alexandria, a representative of middle Platonism, to assure God's transcendence by means of a corresponding immanent God.[63] Nonetheless, wisdom manifests God's presence in the world or that God works in the

---

[61] For example, compare Wis 7:17–20 with Wis 7:21; 7:22 with 1:6–8; 10:9, 15 with 2:18; 14:4 and 19:9; 10:3 with 3:10; 7:21 with 11:17, 24–12:2; see also Fichtner, "Sapientia Salomonis," 130.

[62] See B. L. Mack, *Logos und Sophia: Untersuchung zur Weisheitstheologie im hellenistischen Judentum* (SUNT 10; Göttingen: Vandenhoeck & Ruprecht, 1973), 90–97; and esp. J. S. Kloppenborg, "Isis and Sophia in the Book of Wisdom," *HTR* 75 (1982): 57–84; and the selected Isis hymns and Isis aretalogies in H. Engel, "Was Weisheit ist und wie sie entstand, will ich euch verkünden," in *Lehrerin der Gerechtigkeit: Studien zum Buch der Weisheit* (ed. G. Hentschel and E. Zenger; ETS 19; Leipzig: Benno, 1991), 67–102; or Engel, NSKAT 16, 133–46.

[63] See J. Dillon, *The Middle Platonists. 80 B.C. to A.D. 220* (Ithaca: Cornell University Press, 1996), 114–35 and esp. 127–28.

world through her.[64] Misunderstood by the godless, she is evident to the righteous who can depend on her power that saves the true Israel.[65] Of her, one can say that she is "a reflection of the divine light, a mirror of divine activity, an emanation of the divine glory as a fine, rational, pure, omnipotent, omniscient spirit, which is dispersed throughout the whole world, yet undivided and remaining complete, artistically fashioning all things, and passing on from generation to generation in souls pleasing to God."[66]

Comment 5: The Seven Examples of the Saving Power of Wisdom in 10:1–11:4. A report with seven examples of the saving power of wisdom appears in 10:1–11:4 as an appendix to part A². Each example contrasts a righteous person with an unrighteous individual or group. Thus 10:1–3 juxtaposes Adam with his son Cain; 10:4, the Cainites with Noah; 10:4, godless people after the flood with Abraham; 10:6–9, the godless populations of the five cities of Sodom, Gomorra, Admah, Zeboim, and Zoar with Lot; 10:10–12, Jacob with Esau and Laban; 10:13–14, Joseph with his oppressors and slanderers; and 10:15–11:4, Israel with the Egyptians and Amalekites. In this manner, the report exemplifies the protective and saving power of wisdom. None of the righteous or their opponents is named, but all are described in such a way that anyone familiar with the biblical story would be able to identify them. In essence, as Samuel Cheon has shown,[67] the author employed the wording of the biblical accounts freely and with recourse to other biblical texts. Statements in reference to individuals are generalized; the Egyptians of the biblical accounts are identified with evildoers and, by removing all negative elements, the Israelites with the righteous; and individual statements are reshaped with hyperbolic features. Since the place and proper names are removed, the texts acquire the character of paradigmatic wisdom narratives.

Comment 6: The Seven Antitheses Concerning God's Punishment of Israel's Enemies and Deliverance of Israel in 11:5–19:22.* The title line (11:5) shows that the conclusion (11:5–19:22), interrupted by the two insertions in

---

[64] See H. Hübner, "Die Sapientia Salomonis und die antike Philosophie," in *Die Weisheit Salomos,* 55–81 and esp. 79.

[65] See Mack, *Logos und Sophia,* 106. On 7:22–8:1, see Engel, "Was Weisheit ist," 67–102.

[66] E. Zeller, *Die Philosophie der Griechen in ihrer geschichtlichen Entwicklung* (6th ed.; Hildesheim: Olms, 1963 [= 5th ed.; Leipzig: Fues, 1923]), 3.2:292–93. On her character as mediator between God and the world, as well as on her particular relationship to the pious, see R. E. Murphy, *The Tree of Life: An Exploration of Biblical Wisdom Literature* (2d ed.; Grand Rapids: Eerdmans, 1996), 142–45.

[67] Cheon, *Exodus Story,* 108–14; see also the review by O. Kaiser, *TLZ* 124 (1999): 608–10.

11:15–12:27 and 13:1–15:19, demonstrates that God's punishment of the enemies of his people has its analogy in his acts of deliverance on Israel's behalf. Accordingly, the following episodes are contrasted: (1) in 11:5–14 the changing of the waters of the Nile into blood with the water from the rock given to the thirsty to drink; (2) in 16:1–4 the frogs that ruined the Egyptians' appetites with Israel's nourishment by the quails; (3) in 16:5–14 the killing of the Egyptians by stinging flies and locusts with the deliverance from snakebite by the raising of the bronze serpent; (4) in 16:19–29 the destruction of the fruits of the Egyptian's fields by the hail with Israel's nourishment by the manna falling from heaven; (5) in 17:1–18:4 the Egyptian darkness with the pillars of cloud and fire that guided Israel; (6) in 18:5–25 the killing of the Egyptian firstborn during the Israelites' secret celebration of sacrifice with Moses' deliverance of the Israelites from God's wrath in the wilderness; and (7) in 19:1–17 the destruction of the Egyptians in the sea with Israel's deliverance through the sea. An epilogue in 19:18–22 retrospectively extols the change in the elements that took place in the plagues and wonders of deliverance as the means of God's glorification and salvation of Israel: land animals changed into water animals, swimming animals climbed onto land, fire intensified in water, water no longer extinguished fire, flames did not burn, and fire did not melt the icy manna. This brief summary already reveals that biblical narratives, once again more paraphrased than directly recounted, have been reshaped with the incorporation of philosophical notions. Formally, the concluding section directly addresses God as a sort of meditation (compare, for example, 16:7–23 with 11:13; 16:1; and 13:1–9).

Comment 7: The First Insertion, 11:15–12:27: A Diatribe Concerning God's Punitive Acts. Since God's punishment of the Egyptians is discussed in seven antitheses, it seemed necessary, in view of the philanthropic attitude of the era, to demonstrate that the Jewish God loves all his creatures, is essentially kind and lenient, and thus permits the guilty time to repent (11:23–12:2). As the God who justly directs the universe, he is the God who punishes no innocent person (12:13). Accordingly, by his manner of punishment, God has taught his people that the righteous person must be a friend of humanity *(philanthrōpos)* and that he or she must patiently encourage the sinner to repent (12:19–22). Examples of the gradual eradication of the Canaanites, which they brought upon themselves, and the Egyptian plagues that led to the acknowledgement of the true God in 12:3–11 and 12:23–27, respectively, frame the application of the basic idea to Israel. The charge of animal worship leveled against the Egyptians makes the transition to the second insertion. Based on its argumentation, the first insertion can be characterized as a diatribe, that is, as a popular philosophical instruction. It is formally styled as a prayer. Based on its content, it can be characterized as a judgment doxology with didactic features.

Comment 8: The Second Insertion, 13:1–15:19: Against Idolatry. A diatribe reminiscent of Romans 1:18–32 concerning the unforgiveableness of deifying the creation instead of the transcendent God revealed in his works (13:1–19) opens the second insertion. At the center of the subsequent derision of idol images and idolatry (13:10–15:19) stands a collective confession of innocence addressed to God (15:1–6) that expresses the self-awareness of the Jews dispersed in their polytheistic environment. In it, the supplicants confess their own righteousness as a consequence of their knowledge of God and this, in turn, as the root of immortality (15:3). The passage is flanked in 14:1–13 and 15:7–19 by derision of the folly of venerating idols made by human hands. Its origin is sought in a kind of euhemerism arising from the veneration of memorial images of children who died young and in images of rulers (14:15–31). A critique of religion, denouncing contemporary mystery cults and explaining all evil as the consequence of idolatry (14:27), concludes the first portion of the insertion. The second portion expands the derision of wooden idols to include the fabrications produced and sold by greedy and nihilistic potters and then in 15:14–19 to subject the animal cult of the Egyptians to ridicule. Thus the transition to the second antithesis is accomplished.

Issue 4: The Problem of Literary Unity and Authorship.[68] As a literary whole, the Wisdom of Solomon leaves a two-sided impression. On the one hand, it seems coherent stylistically and linguistically; on the other hand, it seems to have been composed from distinct literary units of varying scope. Although the fiction of the Solomonic authorship no longer plays a role after chapter 9, the sections of the book have been carefully linked literarily. The seven examples of the saving power of wisdom that follow in 10:1–11:4 connect thematically with 9:18. Similarly, the seven antitheses concerning the divine acts of punishment and deliverance beginning in 11:5 develop the theme, touched upon in the final example (10:15–11:4), of the destruction of the enemies and the deliverance of Israel. The theme of divine punishment then finds in the first insertion (11:5–12:27) its fundamental treatment. The second insertion (13:1–15:19), dealing with the folly of idolatry, takes up the motif, standing at the beginning and the end

---

of the diatribe in 11:5 and 12:27, of the deserved punishment of the idolaters. In v. 1, the second syncrisis that follows in 16:1–14 links directly to 15:18–19. The epilogue in 19:18–22 summarizes the antitheses admirably.

The linguistic and literary unity,[69] as well as the careful transitions between the individual sections,[70] gives the book the appearance of a well-structured whole. Nevertheless, in view of the two insertions in the seven syncrises, it seems likely that originally independent texts have been secondarily linked together here. The *carpe diem* song of the sceptics in 2:1–24 and the hymn to wisdom in 7:22–8:1 also seem to involve primarily independent texts.[71] Thus, one must either assume that the book was composed by a single author who utilized texts available to him or, with Dieter Georgi, judge it to be the result of a phased revision of received traditions.[72] Only the brief section concerning the reincarnation of the soul in 8:19–20 and 9:15, which interrupts the context, seems to have been secondarily inserted.[73]

Issue 5: The Adressees of the Book, Its Provenance, and Its Date. The book claims to be a document addressed to the rulers and kings of the earth after the fashion of the Hellenistic tractate *Concerning the Monarchy* (1:1; 6:1, 9, 24).[74] Judging from its context, however, it presumes readers who know the Bible well enough that they understand its encoded biblical allusions, just as they are able to appreciate the Hellenistic rhetoric and the philosophical terms of the book.[75] In terms of its intention, the book seeks to convince its addressees that only unconditional fidelity to the law

---

[69] See Fichtner, "Stellung der Sapientia," 113–32.

[70] See also Wright's ("Numerical Patterns," 524–38) treatment of the numerical pattern within the book.

[71] Other examples throughout D. Georgi's commentary (*JSHRZ* 3.4).

[72] See Georgi, *JSHRZ* 3.4, on 3:11–4:6 (411–12); 4:7–20 (414); 5:15–23 (418); 6:9–11 (420); 6:12–20 (421); 6:22–7:21 and 7:22–8:1 (427); 8:2–18 (429); 8:21–9:18 (433); 10:1–21 (436); 11:16–20c; 12:23–27 and 19:13–17 (440–41); 13:1–9 (447); 13:10–14:31 and 15:7–19 (449); 15:1–6 (455); and fundamentally, but unfortunately with no summary of the analysis, 394–95.

[73] Here, too, see Georgi, *JSHRZ* 3.4, 433 n. 19a; and O. Kaiser, *Gottes und der Menschen Weisheit* (BZAW 261; New York: de Gruyter, 1998), 212–13, with n. 26. See also the reference by E. Zeller, *Philosophie*, 3.2:446, to Philo, *Somn.* 1.138–39.

[74] See Reese, *Hellenistic Influence,* 71–89.

[75] See Reese, *Hellenistic Influence,* 146. Regarding the Hellenistic education of the Jews in Alexandria, see also M. Hengel, *Jews, Greeks and Barbarians: Aspects of the Hellenization of Judaism in the Pre-Christian Period* (Philadelphia: Fortress, 1980), 93–104; M. Hengel, "The Interpenetration of Judaism and Hellenism in the Pre-Maccabaean Period," in *The Cambridge History of Judaism,* vol. 2: *The Hellenistic Age* (ed. W. D. Davies and L. Finkelstein; Cambridge: Cambridge University Press, 1989), 203–4; and Collins, *Jewish Wisdom,* 148–53.

justifies hope in immortality and that the Jewish religion, as the true form of the knowledge of God, is superior to pagan philosophy and religion. Accordingly, its addressees should be sought in educated circles of Hellenistic Jewry and among both real and potential proselytes associated with them. Since, according to the present state of knowledge, these preconditions were present in unusual fashion in the Jewish colony in Alexandria, the book most likely originated there. Should one consider this argument and the additional grounds adduced for this provenance (such as, for example, the Hellenistic-Jewish education of the readers assumed by the author,[76] the derision of the Egyptian animal cult in 11:15, 12:23–27, 13:10, and 15:18–19, or the widespread incorporation of the theme of the Egyptian plagues and the destruction of the Egyptians in the sea in 11:2–14 and 16:1–19:22) to be insufficient, one must join Dieter Georgi in leaving open the question of provenance.[77]

In any case, as demonstrated above, the linguistic evidence permits a dating around the middle of the first century B.C.E., while a few factors suggest dating it only after the beginning of the rule of Caesar Augustus. The position of Chrysostome Larcher, who argues for a phased origin between 31 and 10 B.C.E.,[78] can also be reconciled in principle with this evidence. The political assessment of 2:1–20 and 19:13–17 as echoes of a persecution of the Jews in Alexandria at the beginning of the reign of Ptolemy VIII Euergetes II, as recently proposed by Armin Schmitt, [79] or of 5:16–23 and 14:16–22 or 19:13–17 in relation to the Jewish pogroms in Alexandria in the time of Caesar Caligula (37–41 C.E.), as proposed by David Winston[80] and Samuel Cheon,[81] respectively, may rest on a misperception of the paradigmatic character of the texts, but deserve attention as indications of the nonetheless plausible *terminus ad quem*.[82] Dieter Georgi's argument against the late date, that the modeling of the book on the Hellenistic tractate *Concerning the Monarchy* is no longer comprehensible

---

[76] See above, p. 109.

[77] See Georgi, *JSHRZ* 3.4, 395–96. In this context, it may be well to recall the assertion of M. Hengel (*The "Hellenization" of Judaea in the First Century after Christ* [Philadelphia: Trinity Press International, 1989], 54): "We must reckon with the possibility that much more intellectual development was possible in Jewish Palestine than scholarship is prepared to accept."

[78] See Larcher, *Études*, 141–66 and esp. 161–62.

[79] See A. Schmitt, NEchtB 23, 6; and s.v.; and H. Hegermann, "The Diaspora in the Hellenistic Age," in *The Cambridge History of Judaism*, vol. 2; *The Hellenistic* Age (ed. W. D. Davies and L. Finkelstein; Cambridge: Cambridge University Press, 1989), 142–43.

[80] Winston, AB 43, 20–25.

[81] Cheon, *Exodus Story*, 145–49.

[82] M. Goodman, "Jewish Literature Composed in Greek: Philosophy," in Schürer/ Vermes 3.1:572–73.

after the Roman displacement of the Hellenistic monarchies in the late first century C.E., is unconvincing, since the last of these kingdoms came to an end only between 63 and 30 B.C.E.

Comment 9: The Relationship of Wisdom to Ben Sira. Its greater independence from traditional proverbial wisdom already shows that Wisdom of Solomon was composed after Sirach. The former also mirrors a more developed state of Jewish apologetics.[83] Furthermore, the author of Wisdom abandoned Ben Sira's reserve toward apocalypticism and conformed his terminology as far as possible to the language of Hellenistic philosophy, especially that of the Stoa. Notably, however, despite the common ideal of the inspired wise man, no direct allusions to Sirach appear in Wisdom.[84] In substance, the identification of wisdom and law, typical of Sirach, is presupposed in Wis 6:17–18 (compare Deut 10:12–13). Consequently, no conclusion concerning the early date of the book can be drawn from this evidence.

Comment 10: The Historical Interpretation of 2:12–20*. Lothar Ruppert's attempt to relate the sections 2:12–20* and 5:1–7,[85] influenced by Isa 52:13–15, to the Sadducees' persecution of the Pharisees in the period between the high priests Alcimus and Alexander Jannaeus,[86] which would require dating the book at the latest after the 70s B.C.E.,[87] has not prevailed over the typological interpretation of 2:1–20 and 5:4–13. The linguistic evidence also raises doubts.[88] One can speculate, nonetheless, that the theme derives from the experiences of this intra-Jewish conflict. Thus,

---

[83] See Georgi, *JSHRZ* 3.4, 395–96; but also A. Schmitt, *Entrückung*, 9; and Schmitt, NEchtB, 23, 6.

[84] See Georgi, *JSHRZ* 3.4, 395.

[85] Regarding other relationships between Isaiah and Wis 1:16–5:23, see L. Ruppert, "Gerechte im Frevler (Gottlose) in Sap 1,1–6,21: Zum Neuverständnis und zur Aktualisierung atl. Tradition in der Sapientia Salomonis," in *Die Weisheit Salomos* (ed. H. Hübner), 19–54 with a summary (48–54).

[86] See L. Ruppert, *Der leidende Gerechte: Eine motivgeschichtliche Untersuchung zum Alten Testament und zwischentestamentlichen Judentum* (FB 5; Würzburg: Echter, 1972), 87–89; and already F. Focke, *Entstehung*, 74–86, who understood chapters 1–5 as an echo of the Sadducees' persecution of the Pharisees and chapters 6–19 as a real appeal to the oppressors and who related it to a persecution of the Jews by Ptolemy IX Lathreus in the 80s B.C.E. inferred by H. Willrich, Hermes 39, 1904, 244ff., on the basis of Josephus, *C. Ap.* 2.51ff. (Dates according to H. Bengtson, *Griechische Geschichte: Von den Anfängen bis in die römische Kaiserzeit* [3d ed.; HAW 3.4; Munich: Beck, 1965.)

[87] See above, p. 109.

[88] On the evidence, see G. W. E. Nickelsburg, *Resurrection, Immortality, and Eternal Life in Intertestamental Judaism* (HTS 26; Cambridge: Harvard University Press, 1972), 58–66; Georgi, *JSHRZ* 3.4, 405–6; Schmitt, NEchtB 23, 23; and esp. Collins, *Jewish History*, 184–85.

Ruppert is still to be credited with recognizing the persecution of the righteous by the godless as an echo of intra-Jewish conflict.

Issue 6: The Philosophical Background of the Book. Because of the apologetic intention of the book, Wisdom contains no objective presentation of the philosophical concepts of its time. Instead, it merely employs individual concepts, removing them from their original context and incorporating them in its own system of thought. Thus, it is difficult to identify its concrete dialogue partners. Possible influences range from the Stoics, including Poseidonius and the Epicureans of his time, to Plato. Still, one must not forget the mediatorial role of the spirit of the age.

Comment 11: The Pneumatology of 2:1–9. According to the information in the *carpe diem* song in 2:19, the reductionistic conviction of the mere functionality of the *pneuma* or human spirit led the Jewish opponents of the righteous to an ethical nihilism (2:10–20). The notion that thought is a spark linked to the heartbeat, a spark that flees at death, recalls Epicurean psychology.[89] At any rate, ethical nihilism would be a caricature of the Epicurean doctrine of the contemplative, temperate, valiant, and righteous wise person.[90] The four classic Greek virtues are also gifts of wisdom for the book's author (8:7–8). His skepticism, however, has not damaged his capacity for righteousness.[91] It is more likely that the reductionistic psychology recalls the atomistic pneumatology of the physician Ascelpiades of Bithynia, active in the first century B.C.E., who was influenced by the Epicureans.[92] In any case, it represents a witness to the skepticism and pessimism widespread in the late Hellenistic era[93] that found its time-specific expression in the reductionistic realism of Epicurean psychology. In contrast, it is unlikely to represent a depraved influence of the skeptical

---

[89] See E. Zeller, *Philosophie*, 3.1:432.

[90] See Zeller, *Philosophie*, 3.1:461–65 and esp. 462–63; and regarding the rejection of Epicurean influences, Fichtner, "Sapientia Salomonis," 121.

[91] For the fundamental problem, see also M. F. Burnyeat, "Can the Sceptic Live his Scepticism?" in *Doubt and Dogmatism: Studies in Hellenistic Epistemology* (ed. M. Schofield, M. Burnyeat, and J. Barnes; New York: Oxford University Press, 1980), 20–51.

[92] See K. Praechter, *Die Philosophie des Altertums* (12th ed.; GGPh 1; Berlin: Mittler, 1926; Basel: Schwabe, 1960), 445; M. Erler in *Die hellenistische Philosophie* (GGPh; Die Philosophie der Antike 4.1–2; ed. H. Flashar; Basel: Schwabe, 1994), 276–79; and E. D. Philips, *Greek Medicine, Aspects of Greek and Roman Life* (London: Thames & Hudson, 1973), 162.

[93] See also M. P. Nilsson, *Geschichte der Griechischen Religion*, vol. 2: *Die hellenistische und römische Zeit* (2d ed.; HAW 5.2.2; Munich: Beck, 1961), 203–4; and, further, H. Diels, *Der antike Pessimismus: Schule und Leben* (Schriften zu den Bildungs- und Kulturfragen der Gegenwart; Berlin: Mittler, 1921), 24–25.

ethics of the middle Platonic head of the academy, Carneades (214/3–129/8 B.C.E.). With the intention of contradicting the Stoic ethic of duty, he is supposed only to have asserted "that the highest good consists in the enjoyment of things that 'satisfy the natural instincts.'"[94] Yet we do not know that he propounded any analogous psychology.

Comment 12: The Pneuma of Wisdom in 7:22b–8:1. The concept encountered in the praise of wisdom in 7:22b–8:1 finds clear parallels in the Stoics.[95] The concentration of laudatory predications in vv. 22–23 demonstrates, however, that other influences have also affected the concept.[96] They have parallels in the self-presentation of the goddess, modeled on the style of the Isis aretalogies, in the *Metamorphoses* of Apuleius.[97] Furthermore, the possibility that Platonic or middle Platonic ideas influenced the concept of wisdom as the image of God's kindness may not be excluded.[98] Meanwhile, one can assume that the hymn is influenced by wisdom speculations in which elements of the Stoic concept of the world-soul,[99] Platonic/middle Platonic concepts of transcendence,[100] and Hellenistic Isis aretalogies[101] merge in order to demonstrate the supramundane transcendence of the Jewish God.

Issue 7: The Proof of God in 13:1–9. The same situation can also be perceived in the discussion concerning the philosophical doctrine of God, a discussion that produces both agreement and contradiction, in the diatribe concerning the knowledge of God from the works of creation in 13:1–9. The content deals with the inference of a creator from the beauty and goodness of the world, an inference whose history began in Greek philosophy with Xenophon and Plato, was taken up by Aristotle,

---

[94] Diels, *Antike Pessimismus*, 536. Regarding his philosophy and that of his successor, see A. Goedeckemeyer, *Die Geschichte des Griechischen Skeptizismus* (Leipzig: Dietrich, 1905; Aalen: Scientia Verlag, 1968).

[95] Compare 7:22a with *SVF* 1:159; 2:1009; v. 24b with *SVF* 1:159; 2:416, 1009; v. 27c with Cicero, *Div.* 1.49.110; and 8:1 with *SVF* 2:913; and, for example, Collins, *Jewish Wisdom*, 197–98.

[96] There are 21, or 3 times 7.

[97] See Apuleius, *Metam.* 11.3–6.

[98] So H. Hübner, "Sapientia Salomonis," 55–81, and esp. 71–74; see also Collins, *Jewish Wisdom*, 200–202.

[99] See also, J. Moreau, *L'Âme du Monde de Platon aux Stoïciens* (New York: Olms, 1971; Paris: Société d'Edition "Les Belles Lettres," 1939).

[100] See Collins, *Jewish Wisdom*, 196–202.

[101] See Kloppenborg, "Isis and Sophia," 57–84; and W. Peek, *Der Isishymnos von Andros und verwandte Texte* (Berlin: 1930); D. Müller, *Ägypten und die griechischen Isis-Aretalogien* (ASAW 53/1; Berlin: 1961); Collins, *Jewish Wisdom*, 203–4, and the textual examples in Engel, NSKAT 16, 123–24, 133–34, and 138–41.

and continued to be maintained especially in the Stoa.[102] The objection, established in vv. 2–3b, developed in vv. 3c–5, and repeated in v. 9, that the philosophers (not named as such) stop with the visible and the creaturely instead of drawing the inference concerning its maker, is presumably directed primarily to Stoic pantheism.[103] Yet the challenge of inferring from the visible heaven a cause not identical with it finds its counterpart in Poseidonius.[104] In addition, 13:9 may contain an allusion to the god Aion, first introduced in the time of Augustus.[105] As indicated by the evidence, this god was venerated only in the Greek-speaking half of the Roman Empire.[106] The God who truly is (*ho on*) in v. 1b is a priori for the Jewish thinker the God of Exod 3:14 and thus the God of Israel. In the opinion of the Jewish wise man, had the philosophers drawn a strict analogy, they would necessarily have inferred the existence of a transcendent God, distinct from the world.

Comment 13: Providence or Pronoia *in Wisdom.* It is furthermore worthy of comment that 14:3 and 17:3 (compare 6:7) employ the term *pronoia* ("providence"), while Sir 39:25 expresses the idea but not the term.[107]

Comment 14: The Curriculum of Judeo-Hellenistic Schools according to the Evidence of Wisdom. The question of the extent to which philosophical texts were read in Judeo-Hellenistic schools can only be decided with difficulty on the basis of the allusions that also occur elsewhere in the book, since the author of Wisdom nowhere gives an objective account of his

---

[102] See A.-J. Festugière, *La Révélation d'Hermès Trismegiste,* vol. 2; *Le dieu cosmigue* (EBib; Paris: Lecoffre, 1949), 75–152, 153–95, 260–69, and 341–69.

[103] Compare, for example, v. 2a with *SVF* 2:439, 2b with *SVF* 2:651 and Philo, *Spec.* 1.13f.; and regarding the inference, for example, Aristotle, Frg.13 (Ross) or Cicero, *Nat. d.* 2.95–96; and Stoic thought, Cicero, *Nat. d.* 2:33–37, as well as Festugière, *Révélation,* 2:196–218; Larcher, *Études,* 201–23; Reese, *Hellenistic Influence,* 50–62; and M. Gilbert, *La critique des dieux dans le livre de la Sagesse (Sg 13–15)* (AnBib 53; Rome: Biblical Institute Press, 1973), 13–33; Collins, *Jewish Wisdom,* 205–9, and Kepper, *Hellenistische Bildung.*

[104] Frg. 18 Edelstein = 225 Theiler and Kepper. Posidonius, *Fragments. 1982: Die Fragmente/Poseidonios* (ed. W. Theiler; trans. W. Theiler; New York: de Gruyter, 1982). Posidonius, *Selections. Greek and Latin. 1988: Posidonius* (ed. L. Edelstein and I. G. Kidd; 2d ed.; Cambridge: Cambridge University Press. 1989). M. Kepper, *Hellenistische Bildung im Buch der Weisheit: Studien zur Sprachgestalt und Theologie der Sapientia Salomos* (BZAW 280; New York: de Gruyter, 1999).

[105] See G. Zuntz, *Aion im Römerreich: Die archäologischen Zeugnisse* (AHAW 1991/2; Heidelberg: Winter Universitätsverlag, 1991), 21.

[106] See G. Zuntz, *Aion, Gott des Römerreiches* (AHAW 1989/2; Heidelberg: Winter Universitätsverlag, 1989), 56; and the reaction in Kepper, *Hellenistische Bildung.*

[107] See also O. Kaiser, "Die Rezeption der stoischen Providenz bei Ben Sira," *JNSL* 24 (1998): 41–54.

critical assessment of the philosophers but criticizes them from the perspective of the biblical doctrine of creation in order to convince his readers of the superiority of the Jewish doctrine. It can be inferred from his cultivated late Hellenistic diction that the Homeric and tragic authors customarily read in Hellenistic schools were not unknown to him. It cannot be determined with certainty whether the complete texts or excerpts from them were read in his school or, as Chrysostome Larcher suspects, doxographical works, the precursors of the modern philosophical compendia, were utilized.[108] In view of the known Hellenistic textbooks, however, it can be considered likely.[109] Nevertheless, Hans Hübner's warning against hastily attributing philosophical eclecticism to Wisdom deserves to be heeded in light of the proximity to Platonic statements concerning transcendence he noted and the poor quality of source material for middle Platonism.[110]

Issue 9: Immortality in Wisdom.[111] The term *athanasia* ("immortality") occurs five times in the Wisdom of Solomon. According to 3:4, it is the object of human hopes; according to 4:1, the result of a virtuous life; according to 8:13, a gift of wisdom; according to 8:17, the result of living with her; and according to 15:3, a consequence of the knowledge of God.[112] In comparable fashion, 1:15 says that righteousness is *athanatos* ("immortal"). It is true, according to 2:23–24, that God created humanity for *aphtharsia* ("immortality"), but Satan's trick brought death into the world.[113] Consequently, for the Judeo-Hellenistic author, immortality is not, as for the heirs of Plato, a characteristic of the human soul[114] but a gift of God granted to the righteous. Only the statement in 9:15 that the mortal body burdens the soul and the allusion to the preexistence of the soul

---

[108] Larcher, *Études*, 234–36.

[109] See O. Guéraud and T. Jouguet, *Un livre d'écolier du IIIe siecle avant J.-C.* (Publications de la Société Royale Égyptienne de Papyrologie; Textes et documents 2; Cairo: L'Institut Francais d'Archeologie Orientale, 1938); and Middendorp, *Stellung*, 32; and regarding Hellenistic schools per se, C. Schneider, *Die Welt des Hellenismus: Lebensformen in der spätgriechischen Antike* (Munich: Beck, 1975), 94–108.

[110] H. Hübner, "Die Sapientia Salomonis und die antike Philosophie," in *Die Weisheit Salomos,* 74–75.

[111] See also Larcher, *Études,* 299–300; Reese, *Hellenistic Influence,* 62ff.; and M. Neher, "Der Weg zur Unsterblichkeit in der Sapientia Salomonis," in *Engel und Dämonen: Theologische, anthropologische und religionsgeschichtliche Aspekte des Guten und Bosen* (ed. G. Ahn and M. Dietrich; FARG 29; Münster: Ugarit-Verlag, 1997), 121–36.

[112] See Collins, *Jewish Wisdom,* 205–9.

[113] See Collins, *Jewish Wisdom,* 189–90.

[114] On the relationship of the Platonic understanding of immortality with that of Wisdom, see Collins, *Jewish Wisdom,* 185–87.

in 8:21–22 stand under Platonic or Pythagorean influences.[115] Wisdom's ideas concerning the intermediate state of the souls of the righteous after death presumed in 3:1, concerning their inclusion among the angels (5:5), and concerning their dominion over the nations (3:8) apparently stem from apocalypticism.[116] Thus just as with the other borrowings from Greco-Hellenistic philosophy in Wisdom, the adoption of language concerning immortality proves to be a means of Jewish apologetics.

Bibliography

Editions of the Text:
J. Ziegler. *Sapientia Salomonis*. 2d ed. Septuaginta: Vetus Testamentum graecum auctoritate Academiae Scientiarum Gottingensis editum 12.1. Göttingen: Vandenhoeck & Ruprecht, 1980.
H. Hübner. *Wörterbuch zur Sapientia Salomonis mit dem Text der Göttinger Septuaginta (Joseph Ziegler)*. Göttingen: Vandenhoeck & Ruprecht, 1985.

Introductions:
Oesterley. *Introduction*, 196–221.
Eißfeldt. *Introduction*, 600–3.
Rost. *EinlApo*, 41–44.
Schürer/Vermes 3.1, 568–97 (with bibliography).
R. E. Murphy. *The Tree of Life: An Exploration of Biblical Wisdom Literature*. 2d ed. Grand Rapids: Eerdmans, 1996.
J. J. Collins. *Jewish Wisdom in the Hellenistic Age*. Louisville: Westminster John Knox, 1997.
L. L. Grabbe. *Wisdom of Solomon*. Guides to Apocrypha and Pseudepigrapha. Sheffield: Sheffield Academic Press, 1997.
S. Schroer. "Das Buch der Weisheit," in Zenger, *Einleitung*, 352–62.

Issues:
F. Focke. *Die Entstehung der Weisheit Salomos: Ein Beitrag zur Geschichte des jüdischen Hellenismus*. FRLANT 22. Göttingen: Vandenhoeck & Ruprecht, 1913.

---

[115] See also O. Kaiser, "Anknüpfung und Widerspruch: Die Antwort der jüdischen Weisheit auf die Herausforderung durch den Hellenismus," in *Pluralismus und Identität* (ed. J. Mehlhausen; VWGT 8; Gütersloh: Kaiser, 1995), 65–66 (= *Gottes und der Menschen Weisheit*, 212–13).
[116] See Larcher, *Études*, 301–13.

J. Fichtner. "Die Stellung der Sapientia Salomonis in der Literatur- und Geistesgeschichte ihrer Zeit." *ZNW* 36 (1937): 113–32.

A.-J. Festguière. *La Révélation d'Hermès Trismegiste,* vol. 2: *Le dieu cosmique.* EBib. Paris: Lecoffre, 1949.

G. Ziener. *Die theologische Begriffsbildung im Buche der Weisheit.* BBB 11. Bonn: Hanstein, 1956.

D. Müller, *Ägypten und die griechischen Isis-Aretalogien.* ASAW 53/1. Berlin: Akademie Verlag, 1961.

A. G. Wright. "The Structure of Wisdom 11–19." *CBQ* 27 (1965): 28–34.

———. "Numerical Patterns in the Book of Wisdom." *CBQ* 29 (1967): 524–38.

———. "The Structure of the Book of Wisdom." *Bib* 48 (1967): 165–84.

E. Ricken. "Gab es eine hellenistische Vorlage für Weish 13–16?" *Bib* 49 (1968): 54–86.

C. Larcher. *Études sur le livre de la Sagesse.* EBib. Paris: Gabalda, 1969.

J. M. Reese. *Hellenistic Influence on the Book of Wisdom and Its Consequences.* AnBib 41. Rome: Biblical Institute Press, 1970.

P.-G. Keyser. "Sapientia Salomonis und Paulus: Eine Analyse der Sapientia Salomonis und ein Vergleich ihrer theologischen und anthropologischen Probleme mit denen des Paulus im Römerbrief." PhD diss., University of Halle, 1971.

G. W. E. Nickelsburg. *Resurrection, Immortality, and Eternal Life in Intertestamental Judaism.* HTS 26. Cambridge: Harvard University Press, 1972.

L. Ruppert. *Der leidende Gerechte: Eine motivgeschichtliche Untersuchung zum Alten Testament und zwischentestamentlichen Judentum.* FB 5. Würzburg: Echter, 1972.

———. "Gerechte und Frevler (Gottlose) in Sap 1,1–6,21: Zum Neuverständnis und zur Aktualisierung atl. Tradition in der Sapientia Salomonis." Pages 1–54 in *Die Weisheit Salomos im Horizont biblischer Theologie.* Edited by H. Hübner. BThSt 22. Neukirchen-Vluyn: Neukirchener Verlag, 1993.

M. Gilbert. *La critique des dieux dans le Livre de la Sagesse (Sg 13–15).* AnBib 53. Rome: Biblical Institute Press, 1973.

L. Mack. *Logos und Sophia: Untersuchung zur Weisheitstheologie im hellenistischen Judentum.* SUNT 10. Göttingen: Vandenhoeck & Ruprecht, 1973.

A. Schmitt. *Entrückung, Aufnahme, Himmelfahrt: Untersuchungen zu einem Vorstellungsbereich im Alten Testament.* 2d ed. FB 10. Würzburg: Echter, 1976.

———. "Struktur, Herkunft und Bedeutung der Beispielreihe in Weish 10." *BZ* 21 (1977): 1–22.

————. "Alttestamentliche Traditionen in der Sicht einer neuen Zeit dargestellt am Buch der Weisheit." Pages 34–52 in *Communio Sanctorum: FS Bischof P.-W. Scheele*. Edited by J. Schreiner and K. Wittstadt. Würzburg: Echter, 1988.

————. *Wende des Lebens: Untersuchungen zu einem Situations-Motiv der Bibel*. BZAW 237. New York: de Gruyter, 1996.

M. Hengel. *Juden, Griechen und Barbaren: Aspekte der Hellenisierung des Judentums in vorchristlicher Zeit*. SBS 76. Stuttgart: Katholisches Bibelwerk, 1976.

————. "The Interpenetration of Judaism and Hellenism in the Pre-Maccabaean Period." Pages 167–228 in *The Cambridge History of Judaism*, vol. 2: *The Hellenistic Age*. Edited by W. D. Davies and L. Finkelstein. Cambridge: Cambridge University Press, 1989.

P. Beauchamp. "Épouser la Sagesse—ou n'épouser qu'elle? Une énigme du livre de la Sagesse." Pages 347–69 in *La sagesse de l'Ancien Testament*. Edited by M. Gilbert. BETL 51. Gembloux, Belgium: Duculot, 1979.

F. Raurell. "The Religious Meaning of 'Doxa' in the Book of Wisdom." Pages 370–83 in *La sagesse de l'Ancien Testament*. Edited by M. Gilbert. BETL 51. Gembloux, Belgium: Duculot, 1979.

W. D. Davies and L. Finkelstein, eds. *The Cambridge History of Judaism II*. Cambridge: Cambridge University Press, 1989.

J. S. Kloppenborg. "Isis and Sophia in the Book of Wisdom." *HTR* 75 (1982): 57–84.

D. G. Meade. *Pseudonymity and Canon: An Investigation into the Relationship of Authorship and Authority in Jewish and Earliest Christian Tradition*. WUNT 39. Tübingen: Mohr, 1986.

H. Hegermann. "The Diaspora in the Hellenistic Age." Pages 115–66 in *The Cambridge History of Judaism*, vol. 2: *The Hellenistic Age*. Edited by W. D. Davies and L. Finkelstein. Cambridge: Cambridge University Press, 1989.

G. Zuntz. *Aion, Gott des Römerreiches*. AHAW 1989/2. Heidelberg: Winter Universitätsverlag, 1989.

————. *Aion im Römerreich: Die archäologischen Zeugnisse*. AHAW 1991/2. Heidelberg: Winter Universitätsverlag, 1991.

M. Kolarcik. *The Ambiguity of Death in the Book of Wisdom 1–6: A Study of Literary Structure and Interpretation*. AnBib 127. Rome: Pontifical Biblical Institute, 1991.

H. Hübner. "Die Sapientia Salomonis und die antike Philosophie." Pages 55–81 in *Die Weisheit Salomos im Horizont biblischer Theologie*. Edited by H. Hübner. BThSt 22. Neukirchen-Vluyn: Neukirchener Verlag, 1993.

————, ed. *Die Weisheit Salomos im Horizont biblischer Theologie*. BThSt 22. Neukirchen-Vluyn: Neukirchener Verlag, 1993.

N. Walter. "Sapientia Salomonis und Paulus: Bericht über eine Hallenser Dissertation von Paul-Gerhard Keyser aus dem Jahre 1971." Pages 84–108 in *Die Weisheit Salomos im Horizont biblischer Theologie*. Edited by H. Hübner. BThSt 22. Neukirchen-Vluyn: Neukirchener Verlag, 1993.

U. Schwenk-Bressler. *Sapientia Salomonis als ein Beispiel frühjüdischer Textauslegung: Die Auslegung des Buches Genesis, Exodus 1–15 und Teilen der Wüstentradition in Sap 10–19*. BEATAJ 32. New York: Lang, 1993.

H. Flashar, ed. *Die hellenistische Philosophie*. GGPh². Die Philosophie der Antike 4.1–2. Basel: Schwabe, 1994.

W. Horbury. "The Christian Use and the Jewish Origins of the Wisdom of Solomon." Pages 182–96 in *Wisdom in Ancient Israel*. Edited by J. Day et al. Cambridge: Cambridge University Press, 1995.

R. E. Murphy. *The Tree of Life: An Exploration of Biblical Wisdom Literature*. 2d ed. Grand Rapids: Eerdmans, 1996.

S. Cheon, *The Exodus Story in the Wisdom of Solomon: A Study in Biblical Interpretation*. JSPSup 23. Sheffield: Sheffield Academic Press, 1997.

J. J. Collins. *Jewish Wisdom in the Hellenistic Age*. Louisville: Westminster John Knox, 1997.

M. Kepper. *Hellenistische Bildung im Buch der Weisheit: Studien zur Sprachgestalt und Theologie der Sapientia Salomonis*. BZAW 280. New York: de Gruyter, 1999.

Commentaries:

K. Siegfried, *APAT*, 1900; S. Holmes, *APOT*, 1913; P. Heinisch, EHAT, 1912; F. Feldmann, HSAT, 1926; J. Fichtner, HAT, 1938; J. Reider, JAL, 1957; J. Fischer, EB, 1959; D. Georgi, *JSHRZ*, 1980; C. Larcher, EBib I 1983, II 1984, III 1985; D. Winston, AB, 1979 (1981²); A. Schmitt, NEchtB, 1989; H. Engel, NSKAT, 1998; H. Hübner, ATD, 1999. Armin Schmitt. *Das Buch der Weisheit: Ein Kommentar*. Würzburg: Echter Verlag, 1986. Giuseppe Scarpat. *Libro della Sapienza: Testo, traduzione, introduzione e commento*. 3 vols. Brescia: Paideia, 1989–1999.